CONCERNING
MY DAUGHTER

Kim Hye-jin

CONCERNING
MY DAUGHTER

*Translated from the Korean
by Jamie Chang*

PICADOR

First published 2022 by Picador
an imprint of Pan Macmillan
The Smithson, 6 Briset Street, London EC1M 5NR
EU representative: Macmillan Publishers Ireland Ltd, 1st Floor,
The Liffey Trust Centre, 117–126 Sheriff Street Upper,
Dublin 1, D01 YC43
Associated companies throughout the world
www.panmacmillan.com

ISBN 978-1-5290-5767-6

딸에 대하여(Ddalae Dae-ha-yeo) by 김혜진(Kim Hye-jin)
Copyright © Kim Hye-jin 2017
All rights reserved.
Originally published in Korea 2017 by Minumsa Publishing Co., Ltd.
Arrangement with Kim Hye-jin c/o Minumsa Publishing Co., Ltd.

Translation copyright © Jamie Chang 2022

The right of Kim Hye-jin to be identified as the
author of this work has been asserted by her in accordance
with the Copyright, Designs and Patents Act 1988.

1 3 5 7 9 8 6 4 2

A CIP catalogue record for this book is available from the British Library.

Typeset in Simoncini Garamond by Jouve (UK), Milton Keynes
Printed and bound by CPI Group (UK) Ltd, Croydon, CR0 4YY

Visit **www.picador.com** to read more about all our books
and to buy them. You will also find features, author interviews and
news of any author events, and you can sign up for e-newsletters
so that you're always first to hear about our new releases.

CONCERNING
MY DAUGHTER

The server brings over two bowls of hot udon. I look at my daughter as she grabs chopsticks and spoons from the box of utensils. She looks tired, or thinner, or older.

You didn't get my text? she asks.

I did. I was going to call, but I kept forgetting, I say. That's a lie. I wore myself out racking my brain over her problem all weekend. And yet here I am, sitting across from her at a table without a single alternative suggestion or plan.

Where were you this weekend?

I name an acquaintance I may have mentioned in passing, and tell her I went out for a meal with her. It looks like she has follow-up questions, but she only says, Okay.

You should have made a day of it, she adds, as if to show she cares. There's lots of festivals going on these days.

I don't know. I'm so busy.

I pick up a thick udon noodle to eat with my chopsticks. In my youth, I was a fan of noodles. One out of my three daily meals would be a noodle dish. I still like noodles, but it's what happens after the meal that's the problem these days. How many times do I have to walk around stroking my stomach, bloated from indigestion, and wake up several times during the night before I learn my lesson? Crossing off items from the list of things you enjoy – that's what it means to grow old.

College students come in and office workers flock to the cash register. The din of laughter and conversation grows louder. Everywhere I go, all I see is young people. My face full of wrinkles and age spots, thinning hair and slouched shoulders. I don't belong here. I fear at any moment, anyone could express their very obvious displeasure at the sight of me. I cautiously scan the restaurant. My daughter's bowl of udon is emptying fast. I'm still agonizing. Should I really say it? Would it be okay? Should I not say it? Is it not okay? But there's just one thing I fear: the retribution this rejection will bring.

As you know, I say after a long silence. As you know. A clear indicator of rejection. Disappointment flashes in her eyes.

I know. You're just getting by, she says. Nonetheless, she keeps her focus on me, waiting for me to say something else. I cannot handle the rent in this country that climbs higher and higher even as I lie sleeping at night. Frightening how it grows without end. I've been disqualified from the game of running and leaping ever faster and higher to keep up with it for a long time now.

As you know, that house is all I have, I say.

The outskirts of the city, rows of houses packed in like rotting teeth along small alleys. A two-story house just like its owner: creaking joints, decaying bones, in the process of keeling over. A house left behind by a world that grows more fearless by the day. My husband's only legacy. A clear, tangible thing. The only thing over which I can claim control and exercise ownership.

I know. But I'm all out of ideas, too. Who should I go to at times like this if not you? she mumbles, stirring the bowl with her chopsticks. Her voice rises and falls between resignation and hope. And then she takes it a step further: a monthly interest payment for lending her a lump sum of money. She's referring to the rooms on the second floor with the water-stained bathroom ceiling that leaks when it rains, the grimy, tattered flooring, and the wind, dust, and noise constantly coming in through the old wooden windows. She's asking me to kick out the rent-paying tenants and get people who could pay a jeonse deposit, to secure a large sum of cash.

But getting new tenants won't be easy. Just a few days ago, the housewife from the second floor came down to complain about the leak in the ceiling above the kitchen sink. She said – with a mix of irritation and empathy, embarrassment and hesitation – that it would take professional workmen from a firm to fix the ceiling, not an old neighborhood handyman.

I get it. Just give me some time, I say. But I don't have the means right now. I don't have the luxury of taking on a repair that will cost me who knows how much. I bet the same goes for the housewife who is begging me to get it fixed.

My daughter is tapping the air below the table with her two feet. The heels of her sneakers are worn down at an angle. The bottoms of her trouser legs are tattered and dirty. Is she really so ignorant of the fact that these little things reveal a person's character? Impoverished, lazy, insensitive, and stubborn – such private things, things that should be hidden from the view of others, laid so bare. Why does she let other people get the wrong impression? Decency and neatness, tidiness and cleanliness – why does she insist on altogether ignoring these qualities that everyone values? I take pains to keep these thoughts to myself.

Mom, are you listening? She presses for an answer.

I put down my chopsticks after a long while, dab the corners of my mouth, and meet her eyes. Okay. This is what it means to be family. I am her only family. I am able to be her family. I guess. Because of this house. Because of the fact that I own a house.

All I say is this: Okay. Let's think of a plan.

*

Hey, how much did you put in? the professor's wife whispers.

Her whispers are loud enough for people around us to turn and look. I stop by the building entrance and pat her gently on the back of her hand.

50,000, I say. We give what we can.

The professor's wife takes out the envelope from her handbag and grumbles as she adds another 20,000, Why so much? 30,000 would have been fine.

A cheap rose scent rises from her body each time she moves. Her wine-colored handbag must be full of these cheap products. Things one can easily give away by the bottle in a flourish of generosity if the expiration date is getting close or the quality is too poor. She's given me a few things, but I didn't get around to using them. They were in the back of my mind, but I never remembered to use them before it was too late. Things to remember lurk behind me, blinking dimly as if ready to light up, invariably going dark.

What's the point of giving money when the person is dead and gone? the professor's wife says. It only goes into the children's pockets. It's best to take people out for decent meals when they're alive, am I right? This is the kind of custom that needs to disappear. Tsk.

The professor's wife continues to talk as we push the revolving door into the building and step into the foyer. I step aside to get away from the bright lights and the stinging glare of the even brighter floral arrangement made up of white chrysanthemums. Looking up at the large screen to find the wake room, the words slip from my lips: It's depraved. Depraved.

The late Sung treated us to about 100,000 won's worth of meals. Probably much more. Sung was generous. No, 'generous' is not how I would put it considering she wasn't very well off. Regardless, she always paid before anyone else could, had you feeling beholden, and used it to keep people around her. Still, the professor's wife being miserly at a wake is just vulgar. She claims to be a professor's wife, but she's never said where her husband used to teach, not to mention that we've never met the man. Not that it matters at our age. The lines drawn and walls put up when we were young to separate *us* from *them* mean nothing when we're old.

Because we're all the same old people. And there's only a handful of places that are willing to take old folks like us.

But such things aren't said out loud.

While we find the wake room for Sung, pay our respects, offer our condolences to the sangju – 'owner of loss', or the head of the bereaved – who I am certain is Sung's son, and sit in the mourners' hall, I sip on the mushroom tea I brought in my thermos. The professor's wife shovels down spoonfuls of rice in chili-red spicy beef soup. She eats several slices of boiled pork that's dried up from sitting out a while. Then she takes out her phone and starts showing everyone pictures of her son and grandson.

Hey, do you have a hankie? she says. Or a plastic bag somewhere?

She turns and leans toward me, takes the cling film off the disposable plates, and sweeps the beer nuts in. I help by pulling the plates of food closer to her.

My grandson is crazy about these little snacks. My

daughter-in-law is always telling me to stop, but how can I? I'll sneak him some.

Sure, take it all. I say.

The whole time I don't so much as a glance at the food.

The energy or bad omen trailing from those who have crossed over to the other side of life's boundary – I think I'm terrified of touching it, of getting even a bit of it on me. My eyes meet the gaze of someone sitting against the wall across the room. Eyes filled with resignation. Those eyes that cannot help but see all seem to be marking me out as next. I quickly look away. The game children play where you close your eyes and count to three, and someone creeps up quietly behind you then pounces to scare you. The late Sung went home after work like any other day and died when her heart stopped. A death summed up as 'heart attack'. How much has death gained on me? How did I come to be so sure that it's drawn so near?

A few months ago, the family of the tenant in the second-floor corner room came looking for me. Some people had come by saying they were friends or lovers, but I didn't give them the key. One can't trust tenuous connections like friend-ships and relationships.

I couldn't get in touch with her, a man said. I urgently need her signature. I had no other choice.

The man who came by that day said he was the tenant's younger brother. When I didn't respond, he mentioned the matter of moving their father's grave. Then he showed me a document he had brought with him. As I stood looking up at the second floor, he made his way up the stairs, and I heard the door open. Then there was no sound for a while.

Hey! I shouted. Hey, sir!

I shouted, but did not go up to the second floor. The man came back down after a long while with a stony expression on his face.

My sister is in the room, he said. I don't know. I'm calling the police. The police.

He rushed out of the gate and never came back. The ambulance came to pick up the woman, and police swarmed to the house to ask all kinds of intrusive questions on the pretext of investigating. In the meantime, the man had gone too far away for me to find him.

Did you find the brother? I asked when I finally got hold of the officer in charge of the case the next day.

How many times do I have to tell you? he said. The family doesn't want to take her. You have to get rid of her things yourself. The body will be taken care of by the government, but that's about it. You said she left a jeonse deposit. Well, use that. And please stop calling. I'm busy.

He'd hung up before I had the chance to ask him why, when, or how she'd died. Two days later, I managed to go into the room. At midday as the trees took in the soft, warm energy of the day with all their strength, in order to grow shoots and leaves, there I stood fear-stricken, clutching the door handle. There was nothing in the room I had been expecting to see. Nothing but the routine and habits, tastes and preferences of an average woman living by herself, put away neatly. Death had come suddenly, without signs or omens, no warnings or preparations.

Untimely death, I mutter as I look at the old people at the wake.

If one of these people were to drop dead tomorrow, I wouldn't be surprised. Untimely death? People might jeer that the deceased had lived his share of life. Rather than grieving or mourning, the survivors would judge his life coldly. If he did nothing of significance, he would soon be forgotten. As if none of it had ever happened. On the way out, the sight of Sung's son in a black suit and white armband greeting mourners and guarding the altar briefly caught my eye.

*

They say if you're sick for no reason, it's a shamanic illness. You have to receive a spirit. That if you don't, your child will inherit the disease. Who would want to give such a thing to their child? That's probably why shamans do what they can to take on the burden themselves, I say more or less to myself.

Every once in a while, when I start thinking about my daughter, the feeling lingers: Am I being punished? Did I inadvertently pass on something bad to my daughter?

Jen sits in her wheelchair looking out of the window.

Outside, a member of staff is hosing down the spacious parking lot. The water splits into many streams, hits the ground, and bounces off in clear droplets.

Would you like to go outside? I ask without wanting to take her, and lock eyes with Jen for a moment.

A woman who has lived too long. A woman whose memories are leaking out into some unknown space. A woman for whom the gender divide between male and female is coming apart as she returns to the state of being only a human being, as she was long ago when she was born.

Sometimes, I can't believe the life this small, skinny, insignificant woman has lived. Born in Korea, educated in America, worked in Europe, then came back to Korea to waste her life on looking after people who had nothing to do with her. Never married, never had children, and yet lived a life filled with incredible scenes from all over the world that I've never experienced, and now she lives alone with no visitors all year. I cannot believe she is all of these things in one.

An old man at a table on the other side of the room creates a disturbance. He throws the remote, swearing, and sweeps learning tools off the table. His carer, the professor's wife, is nowhere to be found. Probably off somewhere on the phone or snacking. I get up quickly and move Jen's wheelchair out of the room. I don't have the strength to restrain old men like that anyway.

Before dinner, someone opens Jen's door and calls me. It's Mr Kwon from the office. He calls me out into the hall and asks if I could come in an hour early tomorrow. Some people from the TV station are coming to interview Jen. I tell him okay. Mr Kwon bows at me politely. I think the professor's wife is right in thinking that Mr Kwon is especially nice to me. Not so much nice as respectful. I am not blind to the fact that how he treats me sets an example to the rest of the office staff. Perhaps I should be grateful considering the status of most old carers who work for what is, by any standards, so little pay and are secretly treated with hostility and contempt. It's probably thanks to Jen, the patient I care for. In places like this, the patients you're assigned to matter. The staff are respectful and polite toward Jen here, at least to her face.

How come she has no family whatsoever? people ask when Jen is not around. The professor's wife is particularly quick to reveal her true feelings as if she's been waiting for the chance.

What's the use of family? We all end up the same way.

Very few children make regular visits to see their parents in nursing homes. The professor's wife knows that, but she's not done.

Still, it's different when you have no family at all, she says. Such a pity she's been all alone for years.

When I don't give her much of a response, she turns to the young newcomer who's a newlywed, So you gotta raise your kids well now. It takes work, but they're your assets and insurance. She looks over at Jen in the distance and clicks her tongue, Tsk.

It's moments like this that I feel the full force of my current situation in which I can no longer pick and choose the people I associate with. Talking with these people, sharing our thoughts, and agreeing with them for lack of other options, am I turning into one of those stuffy, prejudiced old bags – as young people these days put it – that leech on taxpayer money?

The young newcomer nods but is unmoved. She's still getting used to the work. She looks after the patients of the late Sung, which is no easy job. She'll have to take a few sick days before her body slowly adjusts. But many people leave before that happens. The ones that stay on are the ones that truly need this job.

I return to Jen's room to tuck her in.

Discomfort anywhere? I'll be back tomorrow morning.

Okay. Holding my hand, Jen asks, Where do you live? Is it far? Or near?

I tell her it's not far, that it's a short bus ride away. Jen nods.

Okay. Watch out for cars, Jen advises. Watch out for cars.

Her saying so is a sign that she is lucid now. I sweep Jen's forehead with my palm. The face of someone who has lived twenty years longer than I have. Her skin is wrinkled and rough, but her features are still pretty. I hold Jen's hand and pray that she'll sleep a deep, restful sleep tonight, and go out into the hall. Jen has had a bit of sleep medication prescribed, so she'll sleep well.

I gather my things and come out to the elevator to find the professor's wife and the young newcomer waiting for me. We nod goodbye to the on-call nurse and leave the building. Loud music is blaring down at the far end of the alley. Just off this small alley is an intersection filled with stores and bars that stay open all hours of the night. The tension of the day lifts and I feel the ache in my knees.

Hey, how did it go with your daughter? The professor's wife asks. Did you see her?

It's night-time, but the air is still hot. Flashes of heat crawl up around the neck.

I'm going to see her now. It's hard to find time, I deflect. I know she wants to ask personal questions about my daughter, pass judgment, and lecture me. I know she's just being nosy, but I can't simply let the things she says wash over me. The professor's wife agrees and takes out her cell phone. She pulls up a few pictures of her grandson.

He looks smart. How old is he? The newcomer manages a few perfunctory words. I don't say a thing. I pretend to be looking at something on my phone, speed up ahead of them, and hurry off the curb to cross the street, saying, See you tomorrow.

Summer nights are hard to get through because of noise from outside. It's difficult to fall asleep as delivery scooters roar, neighbors' TV sets babble on, and the couple upstairs shout at each other. I stick a pain-relief pad on my knees and put pain cream on my shoulder by the light of the TV. Then

I bring half a watermelon from the fridge and eat hungrily, scooping up chunks of melon with a spoon. And then there's nothing left for me to do.

Lying in a quiet, dark room, I reflect on these things.

Labor without end. The thought that no one can save me from this exhausting work. Concern over what will happen when the moment comes when I cannot work anymore. In other words, what worries me isn't death, but life. I must do whatever needs to be done to withstand this suffocating uncertainty that will be with me for as long as I am living. I learned this too late. Perhaps this is not about aging. Maybe it's the malady of the times, as people say. Our times. This generation. Naturally, I am reminded of my daughter again. We have arrived at this point, her in her mid-thirties, me past seventy. And the world that she will reach, that I won't be around for – what will it look like? Better than this? Or more relentless?

The next day at work, I wash Jen as soon as I arrive, put on her diaper, and take out some simple makeup.

Did I ever tell you about when I was in high school? I went to school in the countryside. I had to stay with a friend because the school was so far away. I had to change buses three times just to get home. My friend's sister was living on her own and working at a factory. It was a small room with a kitchen. Now that I think of it, she couldn't have been more than twenty-one, twenty-two then. I don't know why I was so frightened by her. You know how it is at that age. One or two years feels like a big age difference.

Hmm? Where are you going? Jen's eyes grow wide as she looks up. My hand, holding the brush I was using to give her cheeks some color, is suspended in the air for a moment.

No, I mean I went to high school a long time ago. Long time. A long, long time ago. I went to school.

You went to school? Yes, people need education. Need to learn, Jen says.

I am drawing Jen's eyebrows when Mr Kwon comes in.

The television crew have arrived, he says. They're in the reception room. Is she ready?

All the other patients have left for the playroom and therapy room. Jen's expression is lifeless. Maybe she's in a bad way. I ask her this and that, but she doesn't respond.

Shall we? Mr Kwon hurries us along. I quickly apply lip gloss on her lips and nod.

Shall I take her? I ask.

I would appreciate that, he says.

Mr Kwon quietly follows us down the hall and asks, Please take good care of her, just in case. It's important to show them that we are doing a good job of caring for people like her. Good publicity.

I tell him I understand.

*

You wrote a book titled *Children on the Border* in 1989. There are stories in here about children who were adopted in America. Brandon Kim? Or was it Brandon Lee? The story of this ten-year-old boy really stuck with me. The book follows the story of the boy for five years as he is adopted by a white family and then sent back. Did you handle the interviews for the story yourself? And I'm also curious to find out how you came to know the boy.

The young man in the baseball cap adjusts the camera and gives a signal, and the other one pushes up his glasses with round lenses.

Then could you tell us about the LA Education Center? His voice quavers like a thin sheet of metal before recovering its composure. It says here that it was an alternative education center. It was perhaps the first organization for children of immigrants. You singlehandedly transformed the center into an accredited institution and applied for funding. Any particular difficulties you ran into?

The young man's voice bounces around the rectangular visiting room and dissipates. Silence descends. We can hear the careful footsteps of people going by in the hall. All the while Jen's eyes are fixed on a corner of the table. She appears to be in a place where she can hear nothing and see nothing. Maybe she's scared of the strangers. I start to approach her, and the young man raises a hand to tell me it's fine.

How about the counseling center for immigrants' rights you opened in the 1980s? Do you remember that? You were in Busan, not Seoul. Any special reason why you chose Busan?

The young man at the camera peers up from the viewfinders and shakes his head. The two men seem to be saying something to each other through exchanged glances.

I'm starving to death.

Jen taps impatiently on the armrest of her wheelchair. The comment goes unnoticed by the other two. Questions continue as if nothing happened.

How about the forum in Osaka in the early 1990s? You caused quite a stir by speaking out against the Korean government. You weren't allowed back into the country for a while. Do you remember that?

The young man shows Jen old pictures and clippings from old magazines. In the picture, Jen is wearing a comically large pair of glasses and saying something on the podium. In another picture she's all smiles, standing shoulder to shoulder with some white men. For a moment I'm quite taken by these faded pictures.

I am hungry now. Hungry, Jen says. She looks back at me and mimes banging her fists on the table.

We'll go and eat soon, I say nervously, leaning by the door. In a minute, Jen. But could you talk to these gentlemen first? They've come a long way to see you.

What am I getting today? Are we having cake?

I try to coax Jen with a smile on my face as I wonder if it's true what these young men are saying. Did this old, frail woman who's interested in nothing but eating, shitting, and sleeping do all of that? Were the things she did so meaningful that they would come all this way to ask her about them? If so, how did Jen end up at a place like this? Maybe because she did the things she did.

Don't you remember anything? How about Tipat? He's from Cambodia? Is it Cambodia? The man in glasses isn't sure.

The Philippines, the camera guy corrects him.

Yes, the Philippines. Tipat, the little boy from the Philippines. You were his sponsor. It looks like you practically raised him into adulthood. Don't you remember? Tipat. Do you remember Tipat?

The young man's voice rises. I sense their respect and awe drain as irritation and frustration rise.

Looks like she doesn't remember a thing, one man says to the other.

But we have to get a quote, or we have nothing to use.

Can't get a quote when she isn't saying anything.

The man at the camera stares blankly at Jen and mumbles, Look, ma'am. Just tell us about something. Anything. Our boss will kill us if we don't get a quote.

Then he pulls out his phone and makes a call. A high-pitched voice comes intermittently from the phone. The young man glances at Jen and whispers, She's completely gone, there's just no way. Then he says, She's hopeless. What does he mean, 'She's hopeless'? The other young man snatches the phone from his hand and says something. Jen turns around to look at him. I nod and blink to let her know everything is okay. The young men keep talking on the phone in the meantime. Their voices grow loud enough for everyone to hear.

They act and talk as if Jen isn't here. In a way, it's true – the Jen they came to see isn't here. Then how about the Jen sitting before them? Is this Jen not Jen? Are they here to punish Jen? Is this their way of telling her, Look at the state of you. Look how small and ugly compared to your younger days when you were worthy of respect?

Don't you remember this in the picture? Look closely. Here, look here.

The questions are relentless. More like an investigation or interrogation. The young men are intent on getting Jen to say something through any means. They've abandoned manners and tact.

She says she's always hungry these days, I try to help. An hour or two after a meal, and she's hungry again. She's always asking for cake, but she can't have a lot of it. She has trouble digesting. She enjoyed strawberries in particular this spring. These days, she has tomatoes in the mornings and evenings.

I stand by Jen, who grabs my hand under the table. The young men couldn't care less about what I say. They're not interested in who Jen is now. They whisper to each other.

The young man with the camera finally says, almost to

himself, It's dementia, right? We came because we were told it wasn't bad. This is unfortunate.

I find him rude, but I don't share this view with him. Mr Kwon asked me for a favor. If these young men run an article or footage somewhere, it'll be publicity for the nursing home, which will lead to donations and funding. I can't say this has nothing to do with me. I ought to do my part to help.

Would you like to look around the hospital room? See how she's doing here. I think giving her a little more time will help. I'll talk to her.

I try to convince them in the gentlest tone I can contrive, but they shake their heads and leave the room. Their conversation disturbs the quiet hall. I study the pictures and clippings they left behind. I see the Jen I know in the old pictures.

Wow, will you look at this? Oh, my. Do you remember when this was?

I point at a few photos and hold them up next to her face for comparison, but I get no response from her.

*

Somewhere down the line, I stopped believing that I could change things.

Even at this very moment, I'm being carried out by the tide of time. Whatever it is, if you try too hard to change it, you have to be prepared for a real struggle. Being prepared doesn't change anything. For better or for worse. I must accept that all this is mine. These things became mine because I chose them. They make up who I am now. But most people take too long to arrive at this realization. The past, the future, and everything else that isn't right here distracts us as we crane our necks hoping to find something, only to end up wasting a lot of time. Maybe the elderly always have these regrets as they're running out of time.

I don't know how to explain these things. It's difficult to understand something vicariously through someone else's words, without having lived it. This is particularly close to impossible for my daughter, who's armed with strong, impenetrable youthfulness.

Ma, are you listening? Hello?

I nod to show that I am listening, but I don't meet her eyes. If I switch both apartment leases on the second floor from monthly rent to jeonse deposit-only, how am I supposed to afford the hospital bills, meds, insurance payments, utilities, living expenses, and the little extra in case of emergencies? The refrigerator door rattles as my daughter swings it open. She comes back to the table with a glass of cold water. The air is still hot, although it's late. I wave off a mosquito and aim the fan at her.

I said I'll take care of the bank loan interest, Ma. I'll give you spending money, too. I'll take on more classes in the fall semester and have more income. I'm not going to depend on you forever. I'm not a baby.

I nod silently. That doesn't mean I agree, only that I'm trying my best to understand her situation. So I don't pressure her to get by on her own. I cannot tell her what my parents said to me long ago: Try hard, try even harder. I mustn't say that to her. That's how it is now.

Then why don't you get the bank loan for a jeonse deposit yourself? I ask.

The raucous sound of people chattering and the roar of a motorcycle engine going by barges in through the window. She takes a sip of water and puffs up both cheeks with a piqued look.

I hear the government is building lots of public housing these days, I say. Wouldn't it be better for you to sign up for one of those even if the commute is longer?

My daughter doesn't have a steady job. People who work but have no position – the number used to be one in ten, then three, and now six to seven in ten. People with no position are eligible for nothing. Not for loans, not for public housing.

Knowing that this is the reality for the majority is no comfort to me. Rather, knowing my daughter is one of them shocks and alarms me daily and brings down upon me the full force of my disappointment and guilt. Maybe she's spent too much time studying. Maybe I've allowed her too much unnecessary education. She learned and learned, and ended up learning things she shouldn't have: how to resist the ways of the world, how to be at odds with it.

I wouldn't be here if that were possible, Ma. I've looked into everything. I have an appointment at seven tomorrow morning. I have to prep for class, too.

Laughter erupts outside the window. Someone must have left the TV volume on high. I carefully study the anxiety, exhaustion, and irritation surfacing on her face.

Then sleep here tonight. You can go straight to work from here, I say.

Ma, I'm so sorry, she says, rubbing her eyes sleepily. This is really the last favor I'm asking you. The landlord is hounding me to make a decision by next week. I've got no time. I don't have the luxury of looking into anything more.

Why do the things she says sound like a threat sometimes? Why does that look, as if she's almost on the verge of tears, hit me so much harder than her lashing out and yelling? Is she aware of it, or isn't she? She talks on the phone with someone as she heads into the kitchen. Her voice is warm and gentle. Soft laughter. Sounds from her private life I want to pretend doesn't exist.

That child guzzles money. She calls and my heart sinks, my husband used to say. I can almost hear his grumbling now. Still, he was always beside himself with excitement every time she came to visit. She never talks about my dead husband now. Barely managing to get through each day from start to finish, to handle her routine, and make ends meet, she doesn't have the luxury of looking back.

All of a sudden, I want to apologize to my daughter for

my life going on for longer than expected. Maybe I'll be freed from this torture if I say it. Until this house vanishes or I die, this 'last favor' will not come. There is no end to this.

All right, I say, giving in. Let's go to the bank and see about the loan. How much we can get with this house as collateral, and for how much interest.

Thanks, Ma.

Early next morning, I sneak into the room where my daughter's sleeping and sit on the edge of the bed. I grab my daughter's foot sticking out of the loose-fitting leg of her pajama trousers. I stroke her white leg. The healthy, strong body of a thirty-something woman. But she doesn't understand how precious the thing she has is.´

I married your father at thirty and had you the following year, I think to myself. The night I went into labor, I took a cab to the hospital myself. He was in the middle of a desert, and I got in touch with him two weeks later. He called from a construction site in a faraway country. Your name was decided then. I didn't like it very much, but went with it. I took pity on this sad, lonely man who had to wander overseas to make money. I wanted him to feel that we were together now in a solid, strong refuge called family.

My daughter turns over. I look up at the clock and take a breath. It's still early and I let her sleep a little longer.

At night, I held you and imagined this house growing around me, I go on to myself. I got chills as I felt the invisible eyes of an expanding silence looking down at me, ready to swallow me whole. This feeling intensified after his visits once or twice a year. You did not recognize your father until you were five. This man with hairy arms and legs and a deep bass voice made you shriek with terror each time he came near. You would go on hiding behind the sofa and peeking at him. By the time you'd managed to warm up and hold his hand in the street, he had to load up two, three suitcases bigger than you and leave for work again.

Birds chirp outside. The people on the second floor are starting their day with the doors wide open. The young man in the corner room is likely still asleep, so the one moving about so busily up there must be the young mother. A child fusses, she admonishes.

What time is it? my daughter asks, eyes hardly open.

I tell her to get up and come out of the room. I go to the sink, pour a glass of milk, and break two eggs over a heated pan. She comes to the kitchen table. She used to be a small, young child. I think of the times she does not remember. Scenes from long, long ago. But certain among them are still just as fresh and brimming with energy. As clear as if it were yesterday.

She pops the yolk with a fork and adds more salt.

Why don't you just come and live with me? I ask suddenly. She shows no sign of having heard me as she chews on her egg. And then gathers up a yellow manila envelope and some printouts on the table.

We'll talk about it and get back to you, she finally says. It's not all up to me.

I quickly take the dishes to the sink and turn on the tap so as to not hear the next words out of her mouth. The dishes clack noisily.

Ma, don't forget to go to the bank, she says as she gets up with her glass of milk still half full. Call me and let me know how it went. I'll be waiting.

The front door shuts with a thud and I spit out these words involuntarily: The damn bitch.

*

My daughter sprang from my being. She was born into my life and for some time was raised on my unconditional kindness and care. And now she's pretending she has nothing to do with me. She acts as if she was born out of nothing and brought herself up into adulthood. She works out and decides everything on her own and only informs me after the fact. There are lots of things she doesn't even bother to tell me. Things she doesn't say but I know about. Things I try not to notice. I watch these things form a silent, blue-black river that flows constantly between us daily.

You didn't call. Did you go to the bank today? She rings at night just as I am leaving the nursing home. I try to explain credit lines and variable interest rates and loan terms to her. I try my best to communicate to her my conversation with the bank clerk that was peppered with the word 'unfeasible' for this reason and that.

Oh, I see.

My ear feels hot against the phone. I keep getting distracted by the voices of people pouring out into the streets to get away from the heat. Kids who waste and waste all the time they don't know what to do with. My eyes can't resist the allure of the vital hours spilled and thrown away on the streets at night.

Why don't you come stay with me for the time being? I say as if in surrender.

You're really okay with that? she says.

Of course. You are my daughter, I say, drawing the line. Why wouldn't I be okay with that?

She instantly reads between the lines: I will not allow anyone besides you, my daughter.

Ma, she starts. Then she changes her mind and answers in a calmer tone, Then we'll come stay with you, but just for a short while. I promise. Until we save up a little. We'll pay taxes and rent, too. Don't worry about that. I gotta get to class. Bye.

'We?' She hangs up before I can say another word. I wipe the sweat off the phone and try calling her back several times, but all I hear are the long ringtones.

*

I am off-duty on the day my daughter moves in.

I leave the house early in the morning. Houses stand side

by side facing each other, forming small alleys. The man across the alley sweeping around his door says hello. He has a big gut and a receding hairline, but his voice is filled with energy and confidence.

Heading out early today, ma'am, he says, flashing a good-humored smile. I've never told any of my neighbors where I work. But most people know that I work somewhere. I am forced to exchange a few words with him before I can turn to go. That man and his wife who stay at home all day will inevitably end up seeing my daughter and that girl. While they're unloading their things and moving things in, the sounds will lure him out for comment. And he'll whisper what he saw to other neighbors. On holidays when their grown children come by with their spouses and kids, they'll use my family's business as gossip to reassure themselves of their own familial closeness. These anxieties plague me all the way to the park and finally force me to collapse on a bench. I sit up straight and watch the passers-by. They swing their arms wildly, comically, by their sides as they pass. Still, I cannot find the will to move.

I return in the evening to find a car parked by the front gate. A small red car that looks like it was built for a maximum of two passengers. The gate is half ajar. As if it isn't sure if it should open or close.

I push the gate and step into the yard. Out of the corner of my eye, I see someone sitting on the stoop get up quickly.

The streetlight behind them, outside the gate, makes the person look like a dark void.

Hello.

It's Lane. More slender and taller than my daughter. Small, pale face. From certain angles, Lane does not look like someone from this country. More like a westerner with a small head and long arms and legs.

Green is running late. I was told to meet her here. She gave me a key, too, but I thought it would be rude to let myself in.

Lane stands there not knowing what face to make, what stance to choose, what words to say. I slam the gate shut and climb the three steps of the stoop.

Leave your things by the car, I say as I open the door.

I haven't made up my mind about anything. I am not prepared to let a strange person I don't know – a person I don't want to know – into my house. In fact, I decided this a long time ago. And I will never change my mind. I cannot let someone like that into my house.

Come inside for a moment, I manage to say.

It helps to think of Lane as someone who delivered my daughter's things on a scorching hot day such as this. I offer her a glass of water with ice. The circular pieces of ice in the glass knock together to make plinking sounds. In jeans and a white T-shirt, Lane looks three or four years younger than my daughter. The fringe is stuck to the sweaty forehead. Where on earth did my daughter find someone like this? At a time

29

when everyone her age is looking for a healthy, successful prospective husband, where did my daughter and this Lane start to go wrong?

Is what's in the car all you have?

We threw out the old desk and most of our clothes and books. The fridge and washer came with the house we rented.

Lane and I converse without looking at each other, as if talking to ourselves. We quickly run out of things to say and sit in heavy silence. Exhaustion comes over me. My eyes are dry. I close my eyes for a moment. *Tick*, *tick*, the sound of the clock grows louder.

I summon this memory:

Who are you? I ask.

I just asked who you are, I say again, voice rising.

Leaning back against the wall just outside the hospital room, Lane gets up in surprise and evenly states name and purpose of visit. In this tedious game of chicken where both of us know but pretend not to, there is only one prize I want: Never show your face again. Not ever, not even in the next life.

Thanks, but you don't have to be here. This is a family matter.

I raise a wall against her called 'family' and try to push this stranger out. Lane nods as always, but does not walk away.

I came by because Green was worried.

'Green?' I don't like the way Lane calls my daughter that. Calling each other by ridiculous nicknames instead of using the names their parents gave them. Lane's shirt is soaking. I'm certain it's from taking care of my bedridden husband. Still, I don't say a word of thanks.

Goodbye, now. And you shouldn't bother with these things from now on.

I come into the hospital room and close the door. I see a silhouette pacing the hall outside through the opaque window in the door. I keep my eyes on it nervously. The door opens, and Lane comes in. Picking up a bag by the window, Lane tells me that my husband ate two bananas and a yogurt an hour ago before falling asleep. I adjust the humidifier and irately dust the spot where Lane was sitting. She leaves without a word. I sweep the bunch of bananas and yogurt on the shelf into the trash. This is not a dream. It's a memory.

Lane, I am sure, is my daughter's partner.

That memory was from five years ago. Or was it three? I can't recall. Lane kept coming to the hospital even after that. When we ran into each other, Lane gathered her things and left without a word, but otherwise sat by my husband's bed alone, or with my daughter. On the day his remains were placed in the mausoleum, Lane stood within sight, next to my daughter.

Lane. The very same person is now sitting in front of me.

What do you do? I'm the first to give in again and break the silence.

I'm learning to cook. I work at a small restaurant. I write articles sometimes, too. And take pictures.

I can't breathe. It's not just the hot air in the living room. I open the windows all the way and turn on the fan as if to demonstrate that I'm burning with anger.

What kind of articles?

Just marketing stuff. Short articles that introduce good restaurants.

A thick, humid current flows in through the window carrying the news of imminent rain.

So do you have a regular income? What do you do about rent and expenses?

Lane's gaze, searching for a place to land somewhere in my vicinity, meets my eye. A look of someone trying to decide whether or not to answer. Then a thoughtful look as if carefully choosing words. Lane rummages through the backpack and pulls out a book. The large, thin cover bears pictures of colorful dishes and fresh ingredients.

Lane opens up the book, writes something in the inside cover, and pushes it across the table toward me.

For Green's Mother.

I open the book and see the names of co-authors arranged alphabetically. The font is so small and the words look like grains of rice strewn about. I narrow my eyes looking for Lane's name and bio.

I'm here because Green said she got your permission, Lane says. I'm sorry if you were offended.

Listen, I say. My daughter's name isn't 'Green'.

Lane looks up at me.

I know. I'm just used to calling her that.

I close the book and push it back toward Lane.

Green and I combined our savings to come up with the jeonse deposit for the house. We asked for our lump sum back and switched to paying rent because Green urgently needed money. That was last year. So I didn't really have a choice. If I had, things wouldn't have come to this.

My mind clouds with questions. I have heard nothing about how these two went about finding a place and affording it. I don't know how much each contributed and how living expenses were divided. The seed money I gave her when she left home is part of it. That means I contributed somewhat to their lives. I don't ask Lane how much my daughter borrowed, or why. I make it clear that I have no reason or willingness to take responsibility for my daughter's actions.

I'm not blaming Green. We will do what we can to find a way to live together. Even if it means having to throw away everything in that car out there.

As Lane gets up, the sound of heavy raindrops announces a sudden shower. Ma, someone cries. It's the children on the second floor.

I tell Lane, who is at the door putting on shoes, Bring your things in first. Before they get wet. Stay here until the rain lets up.

Without a word, she gathers up their things in the yard in the middle of the downpour and drags the suitcase up the stoop. She looks very upset or relieved. I offer a towel to Lane, whose hair and clothes are dripping.

Borrowing money she can't pay back.

My daughter's mistakes are my mistakes, I think. They're grown-ups over thirty who did what they needed to do, I also think. All sorts of thoughts collide and rattle inside.

A migraine spreads, stretching its arms as if waking from sleep.

*

These kids might be bullies, just better educated and more sophisticated. They may have learned to use something much stronger than fists. That's why there are victims in the world like me who think there's nothing to be done about being robbed and taken for a ride.

Would you like some coffee?

I have to run into this girl in the kitchen every morning now. Lane. I've never said that name out loud.

I'd prefer that we encounter each other as little as possible around the house. Especially in the morning.

Those were the first words I said to her after they moved in. The exchange happened right here in the kitchen, which was thick with the smell of coffee – like something charred but deep and languid. Lane glanced at me and then returned to concentrating on the coffee. After a while, Lane made two cups and placed one on the table.

I have to be at work by ten, Lane said. So I always wake up at this hour. And I need coffee in the morning.

But what stopped me from arguing back wasn't the audacity or the rude attitude.

As you know, I pay rent and share expenses, Lane continued. I paid three months' rent in advance. You say you're uncomfortable, so I'll respect that. But I think you should know that I have the right to at least that much.

Indisputable fact. Incontestable words.

After Lane left the kitchen, I hurried back to my room. I sat on the bed and ruminated on the things Lane had said. Rent. Expenses. Right. My authority given up for the sake of money, my prerogative as a parent, shame and indignity that shakes me to my core. The amount of space where I can rest easy is shrinking. Like folding a piece of paper in half and then once more. These kids will suddenly realize one day that I'm no longer there. This doesn't mean I will disappear; the place I take up will disappear. I will thus become a person who is as good as non-existent. No. These kids won't even notice that much.

After that day, I stopped having breakfast.

And now, I cannot remember what I'm doing here in the kitchen. While I stand blanking out, Lane brings me a cup of coffee and a plate of apple slices, then settles down to read something printed on thin paper as if to say this will be the extent of our interaction.

I know what they talked about the night before. Their

conversation from the living room sofa last night when they thought I was asleep (or treated me as if I didn't exist). The sound of glasses, which I was sure contained beer, clinking.

Should I go back up there? my daughter asks.

Let's wait a little, Lane says.

Can you believe that moron? Family business? Don't butt in? They're all such assholes! They heard what he said and didn't say a word. Not even to the cops! When they all know. They think turning a blind eye is going to solve everything. Are we all supposed to just shut up and keep our heads down?

My daughter is referring to the man on the second floor. The argument between the couple upstairs began early in the evening and grew louder until we could hear everything from downstairs. My daughter simply had to go upstairs and intervene, my insistence that it was nothing falling on deaf ears. Lane followed her right up.

Who the hell are you? Close the door! Get out, you hear me? the man shouted.

I went out to the yard and shouted at the second floor, She's my daughter. You get back down here. And look, it's the middle of the night. Will you keep it down? Everyone can hear you. Get back down here, child.

For a moment, there was silence.

Listen, miss. This is family business. You don't tell me what to do. The man was just barely managing to keep his anger in check.

Your kids are watching, my daughter retorted. This isn't family business. It is a crime to hit a person. Domestic violence is assault, too. Someone call the police! Don't just stand around and watch! Call the police! What are you all doing, standing around watching? You think this is a show? Shame on you!

It took a while for the police to arrive. As the flashing lights of the patrol car awoke the quiet alley once again, my daughter raised her voice to the police as well. When the cops said they couldn't intervene in every small bit of family business and the wife didn't want to press charges, Lane spoke up.

What idiot would press charges when her abuser is standing right in front of her? Don't just sit on your hands and do nothing. At least pretend to look into what happened.

This is a small neighborhood. I don't want these kids causing trouble and attracting attention like this. Whatever the married couple with children gets into, I want them just to ignore it. These kids don't understand how tiring it is to be a couple and raise a family. They aren't the least bit ashamed of their ignorance. They don't know who should be more ashamed of themselves. I see the hubbub in the alley outside, come back into the house, retreat into my room, close the door, and lie down.

After the commotion is over, the voices of the kids whispering in the living room keeps weaving in and out of my light sleep.

It's the easy thing to do. Pretend they didn't know. It's less work to say they didn't know.

That's what I'm saying! People are awful. They're really awful. They know better than to behave that way when their kid is screaming like that. Shouldn't they at least control themselves for the baby? And what about the neighbors? What is this, a circus? I know they can all hear! How can they be so heartless!

Lower your voice. You'll wake your mother.

My daughter's voice is hot and Lane's voice is just cool enough. Cool air sinks, warm air rises. The two arcs make a circle. Mixing the two would make the perfect temperature.

What kind of world do they think they live in? A magical, brilliant place they read about in books? The kind of thing a few people can pick up and overturn?

The phone alarm goes off and my daughter comes out into the kitchen.

Am I the last one up again? Ma, are you off to work? So early? Are you guys having coffee time without me?

My daughter looks over at me and drapes her arm across Lane's shoulders. I look away on instinct and try my best not to look offended.

I have church, I say after catching my breath. You should be getting to work. Don't mind me. I am talking to the fridge like an idiot.

Church? Ma, you still go to church? I thought you said you stopped going.

She sits on the chair with one leg folded up and mutters disapprovingly.

I have never skipped church unless I was very sick, I say firmly. This is a lie. I pass behind my daughter who is playing with her toes and come out of the kitchen. I'm looking through the closet for my shoes when Lane hands me a tall thermos and a small pill box.

This is coffee, and this is a pill box. The days of the week are written on the cover so it's easy to tell.

Lane must have heard me muttering to myself at all hours of the day, Did I take my meds today? I am forced to take these things with me as I leave the house. The color and texture of the thermos is quite fancy. So is the plastic pill box with divided compartments. I wipe it meticulously with my handkerchief all the way to church. They're too good to throw away. If I threw them away, I would have to pay to buy them again someday. A small group of people are gathered at the church gate. I wait for the crowd to disperse before heading in myself.

I hear your daughter's visiting. How nice! In the small chapel, I am too easily found hiding in a corner.

Lucky you. Your daughter must have packed this for you.

The parishioners instantly spot little changes in me. A tall, shiny thermos instead of my usual plastic bottle. A small, light umbrella and a cute purse. A flower brooch made of lace. A new picture of my daughter and me as my phone background.

Her daughter's a college professor, isn't that right?

Really? What an accomplishment. What a wonderful gift. There's no greater gift from God than to see your children do well.

The deacon here used to be a teacher, didn't you know? So she spared no expense when it came to her daughter's education. And how nice to have reaped what you've sown!

When one person starts talking, it's like pressing a button that generates an endless stream of embellished stories. Do they know that I'm not here to offer prayers? Is this their way of silencing me so I can't bring my hands together, close my eyes, and rebuke God for forcing this enormous pain on me?

My daughter is an itinerant lecturer who spends all day hauling an impossibly heavy backpack filled with printouts and books I don't understand from college to college, I want to say, but the words stick in my throat. She bolts down meals and naps in her tiny car, comes home, and collapses into sleep, buried once again in books and writings. The words pound on my chest. And now she's barged in with a mysterious girl who's claimed a room in my own house in exchange for rent, and is out to make a mockery of her own mother. I don't know how much longer I can hold these words in.

Through the flurry of words they're exchanging, I steal a glance at the altar.

When I found out that the person my daughter was calling every night and writing letters to was a girl, I left her alone. This sort of thing was common among schoolgirls. When I

sensed something was amiss with her when she started college and moved out, I tried my very best not to witness any
clear evidence or sign. In the meantime, she wandered so far
off that I could no longer bring her back. It is likely that I
whiled away a crucial period of time when I should have
corrected something somehow.

All I did was sit here in this spot where I could look up
at the altar, run my hands over these words that I feared
others might hear, and let the silence grow. Things I want to
say, must say, cannot say, must not say – I have no confidence
in any of these words. Whom could I possibly go to with
these words? Who's there to listen, anyway? Things that
cannot be said or heard. Words that don't belong.

*

Here. Hang onto this. Just for a little while. Firm grip.

Rolling Jen over onto her side takes a while. Her trembling hands manage to find the bed rail and grab on. Her
trousers are pulled down to reveal a bony bottom. The rash
has spread a little. I remove the diaper and lift up one of Jen's
scrawny legs. The stench of urine and something musty floats
up. I rest her leg on my shoulder and wipe her darkened
crotch with wet wipes. Few strands of pubic hair are left
clinging to her dark, loose skin. The body collapses downward, ever downward. I am disinfecting her entire bottom
with antiseptic gauze when Mr Kwon calls me.

In the hall where people come and go, he says something along the lines of, You don't need to dress her rashes so often.

I don't understand right away.

I'm telling you because I think on the whole you use too many diapers. You could perhaps use less tissue and fewer wet wipes?

Is he accusing me of wasting these items for personal use? Or that I'm wasting them for no reason? But it becomes clear that's not what he means.

It's all money, ma'am. I'm asking you to use the supplies sparingly. I'm sorry to have to say this, but you can get several uses out of a diaper if you cut it up. The other carers are already doing it. You don't need to use all that dressing gauze. Honestly, we could economize on all the supplies if we wanted to.

I am not oblivious to the fact that most facilities handle patients on national subsidy in a different way. When I worked at such a place, I fixated on getting the most use out of limited supplies. The carers competed to come up with new tricks and tips, which the others furtively copied, and in the end, forgot who was copying whom.

But this place is different. This facility is for people who require high-cost care and deserve a certain level of treatment. Same goes for Jen. People in the know are aware of the considerable amount of funding and donations that this facility has received since Jen arrived. The sum she brought in speaks to the hospital administrators' devotion to her so far.

I nod at Mr Kwon, nevertheless. I'd rather not speak hastily and give my displeasure away. Is this about the interview that didn't go well? Have donations dried up completely? Have they decided she's lost too much memory to profit out of her personal history anymore? As soon as I return to her bedside, I open the drawer in the end table. There's nothing I can do anyway. This doesn't concern me, I tell myself as I count the remaining diapers and packets of wipes and tissues.

Is my bundle in there? Jen asks.

I lift out a bundle wrapped in a scarf for Jen to see. It's a collection of certificates Jen received from different places. Diplomas, awards, plaques. They roll around in her drawer with trash. Empty bottles, cans, and newspapers fill the drawer. At some point, Jen began collecting such garbage and now obsesses over keeping it. As if they're important valuables.

They're safe and sound right here. Don't worry.

Okay. I have to keep them safe. They're very important.

A tender smile emerges on Jen's face. Wrinkles in gentle curves appear.

I am assigned to this nursing home. The home pays me on a scheduled date every month. To be more precise, I am a temp from a carer agency. My pay comes from the agency, and the agency evaluates my performance and decides whether or not to assign me more work. This is what I tell myself to get distance from Jen and follow Mr Kwon's instructions.

Squeezing the greatest possible use out of supplies is a tough thing to do. Cutting out the wet part of a diaper, lining the inside with newspaper and stuffing it with toilet paper, and putting the diaper back on the patient feels wrong. The rash on one side of Jen's bottom that was once the size of a fingernail has spread to the size of a palm. Seeing her darkened skin turning red and raw as if on fire, I put the rank diaper back on and pull up her trousers. The rash will turn into bedsores, a dark mouth eating away at her flesh.

The old folks don't feel pain anyway. Their nerves down there are all dead. Don't feel so bad about it.

The professor's wife leaves me with this lecture and a pitying look. Each time she does that, I don't know what to do with the blood rushing to my face. In that sense, I'm worse than the young woman who's only been working here a month. I imagine the other carers leave all sentiment and anything like it at home. Or perhaps questions of beginnings and ends, drawing lines between this side and that, still come easily to them.

Back home, my living room and kitchen taken over by the girls, I'm trapped in my room. The sound of knocking down walls and hammering things continues to reverberate from the second floor upstairs, then the house sinks into silence all at once.

Ma'am! We're done for the day! A man shouts from the second-floor balcony. We'll finish up by the day after tomorrow!

44

I nod to myself in the room, knowing he wasn't expecting an answer.

All of the four months' rent I received from my daughter and that girl went into fixing up the second-floor apartment. The sun begins to sink, and I hear sounds coming from the kitchen. Someone knocks on my door.

I made tomato soup. Would you like some? It's that girl.

I turn down the TV and say as politely as possible, I'm fine, miss. Thank you.

The door opens and the girl pokes her head in.

It's good. Try it. And you can call me Lane.

I gesture her away. A wave of exhaustion hits me. Is it the intense physical labor? I don't even feel hungry. When the girls moved in, they moved the TV into my room. Were they being considerate, or was it their way of telling me not to hang around in the living room? I nod off with the TV on. I think I hear someone come in, say something, and take something, but I can't wake myself up. When I finally open my eyes, it's the middle of the night.

I open the door quietly and step into the living room. *Tick, tick.* The second hand on the clock draws circles. The air heavy and damp, the soles of my feet stick to the living room floor as I make my way to the bathroom. I sit on the toilet with the door open, then remember to close it all the way before I start urinating. The kitchen is spotless. The gleaming white kitchen rag hanging off the counter smells of bleach.

It's not the handiwork of my daughter, clumsy in everything she does.

A few days ago, my daughter raised her voice at me for doing all the washing together. Her white linen shirt had turned pink. She was so angry she almost didn't know what to do with herself even though it was just a white shirt and soaking it in some detergent would have taken the color right out. Instances like this remind me of her father. When angry, she doesn't want to see or listen. There is no talking to her until she calms down. When she is in that state, she paralyses the person she's yelling at.

I'll take care of the washing from now on, Lane says. I should have thought of it before now.

As I stood in front of the washer after my daughter had stormed off to her room and slammed the door behind her, the girl comforted me. I wish my daughter knew how to talk like that, I remember thinking then. My daughter is my daughter. We are family; we'll never speak so gently to each other. This girl and I have nothing to do with each other, which is why we can always be more or less well-behaved and considerate. I left the laundry room without a word in response. Perhaps I'm making too much of an effort to stop myself from agreeing with her every time, from saying a few words in response, and having something akin to a conversation with her. She can be too thoughtful sometimes. It's as if she knows too well exactly what to say in these moments, exactly what I need to hear.

There's mushroom tea in the kettle. I sip on the lukewarm tea that I am sure she made and think, She's good at cooking and cleaning – why doesn't she get married? Running a home, having a child and raising it, becoming a mother and fulfilling one's social duty. Why not take on that meaningful, grown-up role and stop wasting time and energy?

As always, I make sure the front door is locked, and then find myself standing at the doorway to my daughter's room. I place a hand on the door, and it glides open and the rattle of the old electric fan grows louder. I turn down the fan speed and move the bug repellent incense closer to the door. Then I turn my gaze toward the bed. I can't help it.

My daughter, dressed in a sleeveless shirt and shorts, has one arm wrapped gently around the girl who's facing away from her. Sisters who get along well. Close friends. But what draws them to each other isn't something so common and ordinary. Whatever it is, it's clearly beyond my assumptions or expectations.

Still. Maybe.

Perhaps my daughter is mistaken. A misunderstanding between two girls who are still foolish and naive? A few days, a few months from now, it'll be as if none of this has happened? I can take this sight before me, crumple it up, squash it into a tiny thing, and toss it far away. If I tell myself that it isn't true and pretend I don't know, this will be easier for a while. Things I wish I didn't know. Things that I could believe so easily and naturally when I was oblivious extend claws and reveal their true colors when you really get to know them. Truth and reality. It is the nature of the self-evident to be poised to attack us at any moment.

My daughter's calf is slipped between the girl's legs. Skin on skin and breathing as one, they draw themselves together and end up looking like one body. Blood rushes to my face. I struggle with the urge to wake them up immediately and separate them, and carefully leave the room. There are two rooms in the house besides mine. Two fans. Two desk lamps. Two desks. They spend the day in separate rooms, so why sleep in one bed at night? What more do they think they can do besides sleeping with their bare flesh touching?

I can't say I'm not afraid of the things I'll see while living with the girls. Here's what concerns me: moments and scenes that appear before my eyes without warning. Having no choice but to see them. Looking directly at the things I only imagined and assumed, and seeing them for what they are. Things that might be far more awful and scarier than I am prepared for.

The moment will come when things that ought to be hidden will be revealed and I will witness them. Why me? Some might think that there's a reason for it. People might joke in hushed voices. But I haven't found any reason, cause, or mistake that led to this. Maybe that's why I'm being tortured with sights I'd rather not see forced upon me.

One Sunday morning, my daughter leaves the house and the girl leaves, too, before noon. With the excuse of cleaning the house, I open all the doors and windows, and go into my daughter's room. I put her light summer blanket and dirty clothes in the washer and tidy up her desk that's a mess of books and documents.

Petition to Withdraw Dismissal of Lecturers

I find a clear folder of documents. I fetch my reading glasses and peruse the first page. There is a large, square stamp by the university's name. The color is vivid, deep and red; a fresh stamp. I gingerly turn the pages. I sink into thought as I look down at the angry words my daughter or that girl wrote, or somebody wrote, and leave the room.

Isn't it time you started looking for a proper job?

The wording I decide on after many revisions is no stronger than this. But even this I cannot say out loud. Because of money. I know that all of it was precipitated by money. If I hadn't accepted the rent from the girls. If I hadn't taken the extra cash they gave me for tax and shared household expenses. If I could get my daughter a place on the condition that she breaks up with that girl. If I could pay off the money my daughter owes and tell the girl to leave the house right now, I could pressure her to tell me what's going on and dispense warnings and advice with a stern face.

The way things are now, I don't have the right to do that. There was a time when I held that right just by virtue of having brought her into the world. The conditions of qualification are continuously renewed, and I don't have the ability or energy to keep up with it. Same goes for the girls. If they offered me a jaw-dropping amount of money and demanded that I accepted them, how should I react? Money alone can't balance this matter, I know, but I can't stop thinking about money.

Is something going on? A few mornings later, I manage this much cautiously, nervously. I make sure the girl is out of the house before I bring up the subject. My daughter, who was nodding off on the sofa, looks up at me. She came home past midnight last night. It's like this every night. She sometimes stumbles home after sunrise, pale as a ghost.

Ma, I'm tired. Let's talk later.

I'm about to walk away when something catches my eye and startles me. There's a bruise extending down from her temple, scratches on her nose that look like nail marks, and her shoulders and upper arms are swollen red.

Good god, what's all this? I raise my voice. She shakes off my grip as if she can't be bothered and rolls over. I sit her up and ask firmly, I said what's all this?

I fell down, she says. It was just a fall. Ma, just leave me alone. Her voice breaks.

My voice keeps rising and I try to wrestle her up. She catches me on the verge of tears.

I don't know what I did to deserve this, I say. I don't know where you started to go wrong. A girl of over thirty with no job, no plans for marriage, who brings home some strange girl, and now she's out there getting into fights. How can you do this unless you're out to make me suffer? You don't care even the tiniest bit what your old mother thinks, now, do you?

Oh, don't start. It's nothing. Don't say that.

She looks up and meets my eyes for a moment. Her eyes are bloodshot with fine, red blood vessels. My emotions carry me away to a place of no return. Instantly. I close the wide-open window and lower my voice.

That brilliant education of yours, I say. What was it all for? Ignoring your parents and being insufferable and superior around other people? Is that what you learned?

She sits up. Since when do you care about my education? she asks. When have you ever listened to me? You listen to everything other people say, but never, ever what I say.

I've heard plenty of your nonsense, I lower my voice and respond flatly. I don't know what else you have left to say to break my heart, but I deserve better. I have earned the right to see the child, whom I went to such pains to raise, live an ordinary, decent life.

What's an ordinary, decent life? What's wrong with how I live? she shouts. I grab her wrist to calm her down.

What's wrong with how you live? I reproach her. Are you kidding me?

Ma, don't you think you've done enough? How much longer? We've already settled that issue.

Memories of the rawest scene always return. Things I can't come to terms with, accept. Things that opened up and will not close all the way again, that go on inflaming and irritating.

The lid flies open again. There, down the dark, narrow alley, I see my daughter walking toward me. I'd waited for her all day. Pacing in front of the building where my daughter got herself a studio on her own after she left home, I watched the close of day. She returned late at night. She opened the front door to reveal a small, dark room. A futon and a throw blanket. A small floor table and a desk lamp. That was all the furniture she had. No sunlight filtered into the room, day or night. She brought me water in a paper cup. I silently stared down at the paper cup on the floor and left the place. I couldn't swallow so much as a sip of water.

And came the harrowing realization.

If I keep pulling my daughter toward me, this taut, tenuous tie between us will snap. I will lose her.

But that doesn't mean I understand. Or that I approve. I only gave her more leeway. I permitted her to move farther away. Giving up on expectations, ambitions, and something else, I kept taking steps away from her. How difficult that was. Does she really not know? Or is she pretending? Or would she prefer not to know?

Settled? I say now. What's been settled? Have you ever thought about what it must be like for me, seeing you live like this every day? Have you ever thought about what it must be like to see your grown-up child live this abnormal life?

She stares blankly up at the ceiling. She sighs, gets dressed, and opens the front door to head out. I think she's turned in my direction to say something, but she leaves without a word.

My racing heart calms down and a sigh of something like relief slips through my lips.

I am a good person.

I tried all my life to be good. A good child. A good sibling. A good wife. A good parent. A good neighbor. And another life ago, a good teacher.

That must have been tough.

I am a sympathetic person.

You tried your best. That's what matters.

I am a supportive person.

I understand completely. Of course I do.

I am an insightful person.

Perhaps not. Maybe I am a frightened person. A person who doesn't want to hear anything. Doesn't want to get involved. Doesn't want to get entangled. Doesn't want to get dirt on my clothes and my body. I stand on the sideline. I say pleasant things, make pleasant faces, and slowly back away when no one's looking. Do I still want to be a good person? But what can I do to be a good person to my daughter at this point?

A dark silence flows between my daughter and me for a few days.

*

By the time I get off the bus, the rain has completely cleared. I sit on the bench in the stuffy bus terminal for a moment.

The kiosk, the filthy bathrooms, and the ticket booth are all there is to this small terminal that few people pass through. There's a tingling pain in my knee, a sharp needle driven into a sensitive part of the body. I get myself back up on my feet, leave the terminal, and hail a cab in the yellowing sunlight. I stick out my tongue and smack my lips, but my dry mouth stays dry.

What? Tea what? Who? How do you know him?

The old security guard ambles out of his booth and examines me as he takes off his hat and gives it a good dusting. Enormous trucks and stacks of old containers lie on the other side of the gate.

He had a sponsor, I say. That man did. His sponsor is at a nursing home now. I wanted to pass on a few things to him.

Sponsor what? What's that?

My legs grow weak. It must have been the long walk along the country road lined with greenhouses. I'm thirsty and my eyes sting. Why does every factory in this country look like this? Why can't they add some color and landscaping so it looks nicer? Why cover itself in ash color that looks forbidding and belittle people with their rudeness?

Hey. Don't come in here. Wait over there. Just stay there.

The security guard opens the window to his booth and grabs the phone. The scorching sunlight falls over my head as I squat at the factory gate. My knees ache and the soles of my feet prickle. In moments like this, I am sure I am being punished. What on earth do I have to reflect on and atone for? I wish someone, anyone would tell me.

Who are you?

The person who comes out isn't Tipat. The man who introduces himself as Tipat's co-worker looks me up and down and goes back into the factory. A few minutes pass before the real Tipat comes out. He's a good-looking man. He's not as dark-skinned, skinny, or small as I imagined. If he wasn't wearing overalls like a repairman, he would look much better. I wouldn't mind someone who looks like him for a son-in-law. Picturing strange men standing at the altar with my daughter. I know it's crazy, but I can't help myself. He takes off his gloves and pulls down the zipper of his overalls a little. A pungent smell of oil, sweat, and strong chemicals comes at me. I rub my stinging eyes and find I don't know where to begin with him.

Yi Jehee. Do you remember Yi Jehee?

I say Jen's name several times and talk about her. It takes a while for Tipat to summon his memory of Jen. I catch the light of recognition flash across his face.

She's at a nursing home now. For old folks. The kind of place where old people stay, I say.

Is she very sick? Tipat asks.

She's getting on. It's hard for her to be alone.

That's true, Tipat says to himself. She is old.

Quiet words pass back and forth between us in the small shade. I wait patiently. I wait for the conversation to go on and on until it reaches the destination I have in mind, so I can naturally bring up what I've come here to say. The moment comes before long.

Could you come by the nursing home some time? Please come. She misses you.

This is a lie. But if he came by, they might treat Jen differently. They'll at least have to stop with such outright hostility. That's all I'm hoping for.

Just one visit. What do you say? Please.

Tipat's large eyes look down at me vacantly.

I stepped out for a moment in the middle of work, he says. I have to get back. I don't get days off. Give me her contact information. I'll call. I don't have a cell phone, he mumbles as he tugs at his overall sleeves. He sounds annoyed and irritated. His tattered sleeves are black with grease. Maybe he really doesn't have the time. But the disappointment and resentment doesn't go away. I borrow a pen from the security guard and write down a number.

Please tell her I've always wanted to see her, says Tipat. Really. I've always wondered about her. I'll definitely visit her.

When our eyes meet, he adds, I've never met her. Not once.

I write down the name of the factory and the phone number and walk out along the narrow unpaved street. Each time a truck or scooter goes by, a cloud of yellow dust rises, and I stumble to the side of the street and stop altogether. My god.

I turn around toward the faraway mountains. My eyes sting, I feel something in my eye, and tears well up.

How could she do that for someone she'd never met? Send money every month to a child as good as a stranger?

I wipe away hot tears. Sweat and tears wet the back of my hand.

My god. Why did that woman do something so foolish and pointless for decades?

Whatever the reason, the ones who receive never know. Because these things are impossible to understand through empathy or imagination. What it is they are receiving, who had to give up what to earn it, and what color, scent, and weight the money carries in the end. If one had to give something so precious to another person, if one could give such a thing, it could only go to family. Only my child, with whom I shared breath and warmth, flesh and blood.

Why did Jen take on such a pointless mission?

A child who would end up at a factory like this, where he could get no days off, be exposed to harmful chemicals all day long – why help someone like that? Why did she give away the precious strength and effort, affection and time of her youth so carelessly? Two cicadas lie dead, legs in the air, at my feet. A swarm of winged bugs buzz nearby. I'm standing right below a large streetlight.

Why do such a thing?

I bend down to push the cicadas into the weeds. They crumble at my fingertips. I squat by them, and then sit on the

57

ground with my legs stretched in front of me. The road heated by the sun is scalding hot. I sit for a long time. The distant landscape swells and sinks, then swells again.

*

I get home around dusk, completely drained. My breath smells sour and the heat traveling up from my feet has reached my head. I'm at the gate when the professor's wife calls me and asks if I want in on an order of apples grown by someone she knows. There's also a text message gently chiding me for skipping the daily morning prayer meetings. I give each a sincere response before searching my bag for my keys. When I finally manage to fish the keys out, the gate opens.

Hi, you're home, says Lane. Green isn't back yet. She said she'd be running late.

Two small children are sitting on the stoop. It's the kids from upstairs. Compared to the boy, who's sitting on his backpack, the girl looks much smaller and younger. The children are giggling at something on the ground, paying me no attention.

What are you doing here, kids? I ask, and the small girl lifts her head.

Bird eggs, the girl whispers. I made them.

Then she opens her mouth wide, about to swallow it whole. I hold her small hand in my hands and shake my head. Eating an uncooked ball of dough will certainly make her sick. Small children's bodies react violently to even the tiniest of problems. She might have the runs for a week, cry and fuss and keep her mom up all night. Like my daughter used to. Bodies frail and soft like a young petal. But soon warm blood will course throughout them and make them grow in leaps and bounds. I can't take my eyes off of the shine of the child's hair and her face so guileless I can see right through it.

It's okay, it's baked, Lane says. It's hot. Blow on it before you eat it. There's honey in it.

The boy jumps to his feet that very moment and pops one in his mouth.

There's honey in it? Really? The little girl asks, turning the bird egg over, this way and that. The boy looks up at me and Lane, nodding shyly.

Where's your mom? I ask, climbing the steps around them to get to the door.

Mom went to work, the girl says while the boy chews. On the bus!

Bus? What bus? I ask.

Bus driver! The little girl shouts. Vroom, vroom! I rode it. Biiig bus!

It's not a bus, the boy says. It's a van. Not a bus.

I think about their mom's long, tiring day. But then who doesn't have to bear such a burden? I leave the children to their argument and go into the house.

They couldn't get in, Lane says, following me in. They were sitting out in the alley outside the gate. So I invited them

KIM HYE-JIN

in. I'll send them up as soon as someone gets home up there. Would you like some bird eggs?

The house is filled with a sweet, buttery smell. I shake my head. I don't even have the strength to feel hunger. I wash my hands and manage to get myself a glass of water before sitting on the couch. I try to sit up straight, but before long end up slouching. I think I hear squeaking coming from my spine. A burst of laughter from outside. The sound of someone being tickled. Sounds that soar high into the air like feathers carried by an updraft. The sound of children that every home ought to have.

Come and have a seat here. I drink my water and call Lane before taking time to choose my words. It's about my daughter. About the mysterious scars and traces of violence on her body, to be precise.

It might be best if you asked her about it yourself, she says. I don't think it's my place to say.

Her position is firm. I think she's being unduly stubborn and difficult, I finally tell her. That as long as we are living under the same roof, I am trying so hard, enduring so much. So isn't it only fair that you do your part to make this horrible living situation bearable? Her eyes are fixed on one spot on the floor for a long time. Then she begins to speak with a look that says she doesn't quite know how she should go about this.

A few lecturers were fired from the university last fall.

Contracts are usually automatically renewed, but they were just sacked without warning.

I meet her eyes to say, Continue. I feel as if someone is squeezing my heart in their fist. I open my mouth and take a deep breath. What is my daughter up to now? Carelessly rushing into yet another thing that will drain her time and energy, and leave her with only regrets?

It was unjust, Lane continues, I think she believes the cause needs her support. There's the thought that 'I could be next,' and one of the lecturers who got fired was actually an old friend of hers. So they're all protesting at the university. I heard that they're asking people for support and trying to spread the word about what's going on.

I close my eyes for a moment and open them again. The objects around the house blur and then slowly come into focus again. Strength drains from my body, and I feel numb.

Last fall? I think to myself. My god. So that's why she needed the money from the deposit. To get involved in someone else's business. Intervening and making a mess of things instead of simply looking away. Something catches fire in my chest.

I'm sure the university had good reason. Why would they fire someone for no reason at all? I say.

There was no reason, Lane says without skipping a beat. They took issue with the actual lectures, but they probably just wanted to get rid of them. Because they were gay. They wanted them gone. The people who got fired.

Gay? The word rushes into my ears without permission and shoots through my head. Words come to me so violently and without warning. Before Lane can say another word, I quickly manage to correct her: my daughter is not that kind of person.

I wasn't talking about Green. I meant the people who got fired.

Seemingly at a loss, Lane runs her thumb over her fingernails. The back of her hand is chapped white. My eyes rest on the burns and cuts on her hands. I can't take it anymore.

Never say that word to me, I finally say.

She is quiet. After a long while she asks if I have anything else to say, and quietly goes into her room.

I spend a few nights at the nursing home instead of going home. Jen has taken a turn for the worse. Or I need time to come to terms with my daughter's problem. All expressions have vanished from Jen's face. Within the span of a few days, she's lost her strength, her energy, and seems ready to let go of everything else, whatever that may be.

When I was in high school, when I lived with a friend, I studied so hard. My parents weren't so keen on me studying. But I secretly thought to myself, When I grow up, I'll go to America and Japan. Go far away. Like you did.

I whisper, looking at the darkness outside the window. Holding my hand, Jen blinks. Dark pupils. As the skin around her eyes loses elasticity and the wrinkles deepen, it looks as if her pupils are growing darker every day.

You said you studied in America. France, too. What was it like over there? Was it nice?

I whisper in Jen's ear, America. France. Then I say a little louder, Overseas.

Overseas? I lived overseas.

A gentle, toothless smile spreads across Jen's face.

What did you do there? What kind of work?

Mm. There? I worked. And studied. Like here. I can't remember now. It was too long ago.

Was it difficult? Did you find anything difficult? Living overseas by yourself?

I was full of energy back then. I was young. I didn't even feel tired. I did it because it was fun.

I can feel strength return to Jen's grip around my hand. I nod and say, Uh-huh. Then I try bringing up Tipat again.

Don't you remember Tipat at all? Tipat? Tipat. From the Philippines. A little boy from overseas.

Who's that? Jen murmurs back as if I'm telling her a fun story. I whisper a few more words in her ear that might help jog her memory. But I don't know much about Tipat, either.

You as good as raised him. You sent him money every month. Don't you remember?

No, I don't have a child. Do you have children? How many? she asks.

Me? I have a daughter.

Daughter? That's nice. Very nice. She must be pretty. Just like her mom. Her mom is pretty. Pretty.

Silence. While I'm berating myself for bringing up Tipat again, Jen's eyes gazing out of the window slowly come back to me.

Aren't you going home tonight?

I'm going. In a minute.

Do you have children?

One daughter.

No son, just one daughter?

Yes, one daughter.

That's nice. Very nice. She must be pretty. Just like her mom.

We have the same conversation a few more times, then I lay Jen down and pull the covers up to her chin. It takes a while for her breathing to even out. When she coughs and gasps in her sleep once in a while, I quietly get up and adjust the angle of her bed. No one has come to replace the old man, her former roommate, who died a few months ago. This room costs more than the others.

I think I sent her to school for too long. My daughter, I mean. I wanted her to get all the education she wanted. Go to college, go to grad school, become a professor, and find a good husband. But you know what? My daughter turned out to be an idiot. I don't know what she could be thinking. Just the thought of her stops my heart these days. It's my fault, isn't it? I must have done something wrong. Me. But I really can't figure it out. Where do I begin with her? Can I even handle it? But I'm still her mother. Who on earth will do it, if not me?

Something tips over in my heart, disturbing the calm and creating waves. I take a deep breath. Outside the window, something glittery soars into the sky. A plane.

It breaks my heart. Why won't she try to live a normal life? Why won't she even try? Why did I bring a child like that into the world? And to think how happy I was when I first had her! She was a wonder to look at and gazing down at the sleeping child filled me with feelings I can only describe as love.

I stop for a moment and click my teeth together as if to cut myself off. Some words I simply cannot say out loud. They're driven in like iron spikes that will never come out. Why does my daughter, of all people, have to like women? She is throwing at me this problem that other parents never, ever have to trouble themselves with for as long as they live, coercing me and bullying me to get over it. How could she be so cruel? Why am I ashamed of this child that came out of me? I don't like the fact that I am ashamed to be her mother. Why is she making me deny her, and by extension myself and this entire life I've lived?

I've all but fallen asleep when the phone rings. My daughter's animated voice carries through the receiver.

Ma, where are you? You said you were sleeping at the hospital tonight? Lane told me. Isn't it uncomfortable over there? Are you okay?

She's talking as if nothing happened. I hear faint music over the din of people talking all at once in the background.

What time is it? Where are you?

I quietly come out of the room and walk over to the emergency stairs.

What do you mean, where am I? I'm at home, of course. Hey, what time is it? My daughter asks someone near her. What? Really? Oh, no, the buses have stopped running! Why don't you just sleep here? Of course, it's okay. Stay here for the night.

Didn't you say you were home? Who are all these people? Who did you bring home? My heart starts to pound. Who on earth did she bring home at this hour? What commotion are they planning in this neighborhood that falls as silent as the grave at night? What if someone sees? What if strange accounts travel from household to household, embellished and altered at every stop, sweeping through the neighborhood? What if the words reach my ears like a storm?

Oh, they're just friends, she says. They stopped by to pick something up and got delayed. Ma, it's uncomfortable over there at the hospital. Can you even sleep there? And by the way, is it okay if my friends stay over for the night? They'll leave first thing in the morning anyway. I honestly lost track of the time.

I sit in one corner of the stairwell. Do I reason with her? Or implore? Or scold? Or say nothing? I tell her I'll stop by in the morning and hang up. I toss and turn until dawn breaks outside.

By the time I turn into the alley, it's completely bright out. I'm afraid the man opposite might suddenly emerge from his house. I'm on edge for reasons I don't understand, and it doesn't let up until I open the gate. The iron gate swings with a startlingly loud noise. The front door is ajar. The windows are wide open as well. Did they fall asleep without locking up? Why are these kids so careless?

Ma?

I'm looking at the shoes cluttering the entrance when my daughter comes running out. Before I can get a word in, a bunch of people follow her out from the kitchen, along with a spicy, nutty smell of food. Three women, two men, and Lane. The living room fills up instantly.

Hi, we're sorry we barged in like this. We were kind of out of sorts yesterday.

A woman in thick glasses says hello and everyone else follows suit. Trousers rolled up to their knees, these people are wide awake and enthusiastic at this early hour. There's a long piece of cloth stretched across the living room with wooden panels, colorful paper, and fliers strewn around it.

No worries. Make yourselves at home, I say and head for my room, but they lead me into the kitchen. I am seated in one of the four chairs. Fluffy steamed egg and boiled potatoes, tomato and broccoli stir-fry, cucumber and lettuce salad, crunchy toast. There's also ramen cooked with lots of peppers. I'm not particularly hungry, but I taste the food that I'm sure Lane made.

Isn't it good? You don't notice when you're eating, but it's the kind of taste you end up craving later, says the man sitting across from me as he takes a bite of his toast.

You haven't been to Lane's restaurant, have you? Where is it? Anyway, it's turning into a real hot spot. Foreigners go there to eat, too, the woman in glasses chimes in.

I listen to their conversations in silence. And I wonder how they see my daughter and this girl. I also wonder what kind of people my daughter and this girl are associating with. My daughter silently stands by the table and chomps on a long piece of cucumber, brow knitted, deep in thought. She's mouthing something back and forth with Lane. The red mark on her neck is still there. What in God's name is she up to?

Me? I work at a research center. She's a reporter. Works full-time at an NGO. Elementary school teacher.

I'm surprised to find that some of them are married. People with jobs and families. What has possessed them to take an interest in these things that have nothing to do with them? What does it have to do with them? I feel exposed. I don't know what face to make or what to say. I cannot just be myself around these people in the way I felt comfortable around my daughter's friends long ago.

How do you find the time? I say. They don't hear the hidden meaning behind my words. They toss around various responses between them that sound like compliments or excuses, then leave the table one by one. Lane is the last one remaining.

We have some leftovers. Would you like me to pack you a lunch? Lane asks as she clears the table. I shake my head. I rush out of the house and keep walking for a while before thinking back to what just happened there. The voices of many people varying in tone and timbre settled in every corner of the house, clearing out the silence and breathing life into it. The house stretching its sleepy limbs and becoming a home. Maybe that's what I just saw back there. The house bustling with people coming and going. What I wish I had every now and then.

But these people are good friends and colleagues only for now. People who could turn their backs on you at any moment. What I need in my home now isn't people who can leave at any time, but family. That's the only thing that will protect my daughter. Where do I even begin explaining something so obvious and irrefutable to her?

*

The ward is stirred up this morning. It's the fortnightly bath day. Some time ago, a carer fell down trying to hold up an old patient by herself. The old patient shattered his knees and elbows irreparably. The family came and raged at the staff while the nurses went to every room and told the carers to keep their mouths shut about what happened. In the end, the situation was settled by firing the carer at the end of the day.

The young newcomer is in charge of the entire room next door. Four patients to a carer. The workload is impossible considering I look after Jen only. I search the hall up and down for the professor's wife, give up, and ask the newcomer for help.

Can't you move her by yourself? The newcomer says as she pulls down a male patient's trousers and changes his diaper. She puts a plastic bag over his penis and ties it in place with a rubber band, and puts a half-piece of diaper on him. I wonder if the plastic bag is really necessary, but I don't say anything as I look away. I cannot blame her. I coax the disgruntled newcomer to Jen's room to find it empty. I pick up the hospital shirt and sheets off the floor and call Jen. She isn't in any of the rooms or the halls.

You should have at least tied her hands down, the newcomer says. Call me when you find her.

The newcomer goes back to her patients, and at long last I find Jen in the first-floor laundry room. She is leaning against the long window looking out.

There you are. I've been looking for you. What are you doing here?

Jen slowly backs away from me. She's holding something in her hand. The cart carrying empty food trays rattles noisily as it goes by in the hall. I reach out toward her and approach, one cautious step at a time.

It's time for your bath. Let's go.

When I finally grab Jen's hand, I slip and nearly fall. The wide legs of Jen's hospital trousers are getting wet, and the floor is flooding. I snatch the thing Jen is holding in her hand. It's a half-piece diaper. The shelf and floor below the window are already messy with the urine and excrement from her diaper.

Stark naked, Jen manages to stand up hanging onto the bar installed by the sink. Loose feces run down from Jen's buttocks to her thighs and calves. This isn't the first time it's happened, but I clench my jaw and mumble through my teeth, It's horrifying. Just horrifying.

Hang on. I'll make it quick.

I hose down Jen with the showerhead.

No. I don't want to.

Soft flesh devoid of elasticity hangs wearily off her sickly bones. Loose skin flaps together as I lather. Jen's legs are shaking. I wash her thoroughly between the legs with soapy hands and remove the dead skin around her bedsore.

Why live this long, Jen? I think to myself.

In moments like this, I'm brought face to face with the ruthlessness of life. One hill after another after another. Climbing at first with hope and then gradually in resignation. But life never goes easy. A foe without mercy or magnanimity. A losing battle. A fight that ends only with defeat.

Jen loses her balance. I hold her instinctively. Wrinkled like a deflated balloon, Jen is heavier than I expected. Maybe it's the weight of time and memories accumulated over the years, not bones, flesh, fat, or water. Maybe it's proof that she still has warm blood circulating through her body. In this way, I keep trying to remind myself that Jen is still a person.

Hold yourself up. Up you get. Use your legs.

Jen grasps me around the neck even harder. I can't imagine where all this strength is coming from. I can't breathe. When I try to push her away on impulse, she bites down on my neck.

Ow! Ow! You're hurting me!

The louder I shout, the harder Jen resists. She grabs my hair in both hands and clings to me. Her rough, hot breath is deafening in my ear. The showerhead dances and sprays water everywhere.

I am going to die. I really think this is how I am going to die, I think to myself. The bathroom door flies open and someone rushes in.

Oh! Oh, heavens!

It's the cook. The woman in the white gown shifts from foot to foot not knowing what to do, and then runs down the hallway calling the nurses.

*

I stand in the middle of a street crowded with young people. The heat of midsummer threatens to melt the pavement slabs.

Buildings look as if they are swaying from side to side in the heat and my vision blurs.

Which way from here?

If I ask myself, my slow, fumbling mind offers no answer. I have no other option besides asking someone to stop and help me. This is like standing at the curb waving my arm for a cab that will not pull in for me. Maybe harder. Fortunately, a girl in yellow sneakers fans herself as she points in the direction of the underpass.

Beyond the other side of the dark, cool underpass, I see the main gate of the university. The palm of my hand sticks to my clammy skin each time I wipe my sweat in the humid, hot summer weather that saps a person's energy. I let myself sag onto a bench by a kiosk with a view of the main gate.

Please sign the petition. Show us your support.

At the gate across the street, people stand behind a folding table shouting to get people's attention. There's even a poorly pitched tent behind them. The sun gets in my eyes and I can't make out the words on the banner.

Would you like a cold bottle of water? the woman in the kiosk cranes her neck and asks. Her way of telling me to buy something or get off her bench. I nod and give her a thousand-won note. The water is half-frozen. I take one sip, then another, hold it in my mouth for a moment, and swallow. A group of people who appear to be tourists stand in a circle, beckon each other, and make a racket before crossing the street. The tourists blocking my view move away, and I can once again see the people shouting something as they hand out fliers.

They've been at it all day with the sun beating down on them. Such stamina, the woman in the kiosk mumbles as she bows her way out of the small side door. There's people like that everywhere these days. I was at the district office the other day, and there was a big hoopla there, too. So much complaining and fussing. The problem is, people think that someone will listen to their bellyaching. They ought to learn to be grateful.

The kiosk woman taps the bench with her fan and sits down next to me. A chirp of cicadas comes and goes like cloudburst, starting with something like the whirr of an engine and escalating to a horrific, piercing screech like claws scraping at a metal surface. The noise gone, a sense of calm settles in my heart like vertigo.

It's reassuring to see these little shops are around in these hard times, I say, managing to change the subject. My eyes are still on the people across the street. A long row of buses pull up at the bus stop and continue on their way one after another like a long train.

You don't make a fortune sitting in this hole, I can tell you that. Too many convenience stores nearby. All I get is delivery guys on scooters popping in for a pack of cigarettes. Still, I'm grateful when I think of people who are worse off. Stay positive, you see?

The city granted permits to a small number of vendors

who'd been living off illegal kiosks for many years. This was a few years ago. Thanks to that, some people came to own kiosks. They were maybe three square meters, but reportedly went for 100 to 200 million won. The woman keeps talking. Her stories keep stretching further back into the past – stories meaningful only to her.

We weren't like that, when we were young. We didn't complain about what we couldn't have and were grateful for what we were given. We could live without law. But people these days are always nagging and arguing. They're throwing away their precious time on the streets.

I nod, give her a sincere enough response, and try to empathize.

What are they saying, anyway? I ask after a long silence. Fortunately, the woman doesn't detect my complicated feelings hidden behind the nonchalant tone.

I don't know. The university apparently fired some lecturers without a shred of explanation. But times are hard for everyone these days. Even universities can't feed everyone, don't you think? Another group of people did something similar before, and the police poured into the university campus and everything. Huge chaos. What's the world coming to? Someone's always sitting out there. I'm not even curious anymore.

After a long silence I manage to say, Still, it's not right to fire someone without cause.

Disturbing peace like that all the time isn't right, either.

Refusing to hear the other person out, as if their side of the story is the only thing that matters.

I nod half-heartedly and continue to sit on the bench. The water turns lukewarm and I think I'll turn into a puddle on the spot.

Please don't ignore us! Give us your support!

Someone who looks like my daughter, who could be my daughter, is waving her arms over her head trying to rally support. Sunset spreads along the horizon. The tired, forlorn colors extend over the campus inside the gates. I see that the prime of my life has gone. Where I stand, the times I live in, and the things I see – they remind me of the wonderful moments in my life that I can never get back to.

There was a time when my child thought that her mother was her entire universe. Took my words in like a sponge. When I said something was wrong, she understood it was wrong. When I said something was right, it was right to her. A child who would apologize when chastised and quickly return to the correct path. My child has raced far ahead of me. Picking up a switch and making a stern face doesn't work. Her world is so far away from mine. She will never return to my arms.

Maybe it's my fault.

I cannot shake this suspicion. Over time it turns to guilt. I am speechless as I observe the rise and fall of emotions, each with their own colors and patterns. The expectations and ambitions, possibilities and hopes concerning my daughter – they still remain and torment me no matter how hard I work to get rid of them. To be rid of them, how skeletal and empty do I have to be?

I get up. Each time a bus stops, a group of students get off and get on. I stand at the light unable to decide if I should cross the street, trace my steps back home, or get on the bus. The light turns green, people cross, the light turns red again. Cars run over my shadow as they zip by. On my way to the bus stop, I quickly snatch up a few fliers that have fallen on the ground and put them in my purse. But as one day passes and then another, I keep them folded into a small wedge in my bag.

*

Aah! Open wide! Aah, aah! The professor's wife cries out as she helps an elderly man brush his teeth. He keeps swallowing his toothpaste.

No, spit it out! Don't you understand anything? Spit. Patooey! Like this!

The professor's wife presses the old man's head down to get him to spit. The old man gasps and hacks. I turn the words over in my head for some time and finally manage to speak. Could she spare some of her antiseptic gauze and diapers?

We have two more weeks to go, the professor's wife says

as she pulls me by the arm to a corner of the hospital room. You're out already? All of it?

I give her hand a big squeeze and let go, my way of keeping my mouth shut. We're always short, they never give us enough supplies, and it's not as if I don't know how to make them last. Only, I can't bring myself to do it.

What can I say? I did the best I could. Please, anything you can spare.

The professor's wife eyes me suspiciously. I don't tell her that Jen's bottom has a dark hole that looks as if she's been shot. I also don't tell her that it's going to get bigger and bigger every day until it swallows her whole. Whatever I tell her, the professor's wife is going to think it has nothing to do with her. She will think that it'll be a long, long time before this becomes her reality, and so will think she's got nothing to do with it. How can she be so foolish? Why does she refuse to see anything, whatever it is, until it appears before her in the flesh? Like my daughter and that girl.

I get three diapers and half a box of antiseptic gauze from her, and peel the wet diaper off Jen's bottom. The stench of urine permeates the room. I pull back the lifeless flesh and wipe her around the crotch and anus. The bedsore has grown. I open the window, come back to Jen's side, and leave her trousers down for a while.

Does it hurt? Does it itch? I ask.

Jen is unresponsive as she holds onto the railing with her back turned. The flesh is rotting and the nerves are dying. A commotion erupts out in the hall. An old man with advanced dementia is yelling that he wants to go home. The nurses and carers block his way and raise their voices at him. Sound of scuffles continue, then a mournful tune carries over the hubbub. It must be the old man who traveled all over the country singing in a folk show troupe. Small frame, boundless energy. He begs anyone passing by to put stage makeup on him, and when made up, breaks into a loud song. In moments like this, the old man is transformed from a patient waiting for death to a person with memories and talent who is still capable of something.

That's good. Nice voice. Who's singing? Jen whispers, rolling over to my side. She seems to have forgotten all about the incident in the bathroom a few hours ago. Her eyes meet mine, which were looking down at the crumpled flier. She instantly sees that I've been sniffling like an idiot. Jen doesn't say a word. She only extends her hand and passes me a handkerchief from by her head.

Some parents threaten their children. They put a bottle of pesticide in front of them and suggest they drink it and die together. Some actually kill their children and die with them. I'm not saying I understand. I am only thinking of the emotions that they must have been overwhelmed by at the time. What drives people to such drastic action? What uncontrollable emotions push someone to that point?

*

Ma, I'm just calling an unfair thing unfair. What's bad about pointing out something that's wrong? Is that a bad thing? Is it? Why is that bad?

My daughter comes home around midnight. Her breath smells ripe. I am looking down at the flier on the kitchen table. There is a tear halfway up along the middle where the paper was creased. The rain comes down outside noisily. The windows closed, the air inside the house is heavy and wet.

Are you having fun standing in the heat putting on a show? I speak as softly as possible. Revealing your name and face for everyone to see? You think it's right to go around with people like you and behave like children?

You were there? When?

She looks surprised. I see her mark extending from the bottom of her ear down along her neck. A soft click of the latch comes from the other side of the house where Lane hurriedly closes the door. Something flashes in my head as if a light has been switched on.

I threw away my job and everything to raise you. I was nervous about leaving you in someone else's care, so I gave up on one thing and then another until I had nothing left. Do you know what I went through to raise you? You were my entire world. Good god! And here you are disappointing me and breaking my heart with every little thing you do. You wouldn't be doing this to me unless you were out to destroy me.

I know, Ma. I know so very well what you went through

to raise me. That's why I'm doing the best I can. What more do you want from me?

The best you can?

My heart stops. I take a deep breath and continue.

Making trouble everywhere you go. Always complaining. Always blaming your problems on someone else. That's the best you can do? Will you just look at how other people are living? No one lives like you do. Sure, your generation is known to be strong-willed, but just look at yourself! You treat me like I'm a backward old hag when I advise you to come to your senses. Like it's impossible to have a discussion with me. But that's not what I'm trying to get you to realize. You think you're going to be young forever? You think you can screw up all you want and you'll still have all the time in the world to set things right?

My daughter's face crumples.

When people say something can't be done, there's always a good reason for it. So why keep shouting in the streets that it's wrong? Why do you of all people have to do it? If something is wrong, it'll right itself naturally. Why drain yourself fighting for strangers who have nothing to do with you? You bring home some girl who has no job, who God knows where she's been, you get into fistfights with people, you waste your time at the school gate dressed like a hobo instead of going to teach – why are you wasting your precious life?

Don't talk to me that way, she says.

Why are you doing this? I cut her off. Sure, you've liked

to stand out since you were a kid. You wanted to do things that other kids found too difficult or uncomfortable. I shouldn't have praised and encouraged you. I should have scolded and disciplined you. Look here. This isn't one of those things. You are not a baby anymore. Why would anyone do something so absurd for just a few words of praise?

You think I'm enjoying this?

It's not too late. Find yourself someone decent and get married. Have kids. Everyone makes mistakes when they're young. You still have time to set it right. I am your mother. Who will say these things to you if not me? No one else cares or minds how you live your life.

I feel so many memories that have nothing to do with this moment quicken and well up. I massage my aching knees and neck to distract myself from them. But Jen's face inserts itself. I hear her heavy breathing, the smell of urine and something else nauseating.

I am your mother. Youth is fleeting. You will be forty before you know it, then fifty, then you're old. Are you going to spend your life alone like this?

In this way, I refer to Jen without naming her. A woman growing old in confined, suffocating solitude. A pitiful, unfortunate person who must face the dusk of her life alone after wasting her youth and every last drop of herself on others, society, and other equally grand things. The thought of my daughter meeting the same fate as Jen is enough to stop my heart.

Ma, this isn't someone else's business. It's my business. It could happen to me, too, at any time. And I'm not alone.

There must be a thick, enormous, invisible wall between my daughter and me. That must be why I could scream and scream from where I stand and she'd never hear me. Long ago, around the time my daughter first entered college, we had a similar argument. It was provoked by her sudden announcement that she would be going to some place in Africa to volunteer. That was not the first time she had dashed my hopes that she would grow up to be a civil servant or a teacher, but I tore into her nevertheless. Why such a dangerous place? Why now? Why my daughter? I remember saying such things. I also remember giving her some extra cash on the morning she left for her volunteer trip and encouraging her to work hard on studying for the civil service or teacher certificate exam when she returned. She came back at the end of her summer vacation and moved out of the house in the following spring. She declared herself independent in a way that I had never imagined or agreed to.

The day she left home, I sat down to eat with my husband and finished two bowls of rice on the spot. Then I threw it all back up and spent the night suffering from a violent stomach ache. The body reflecting the heart. Telling myself that my daughter was dead to me, I felt a sense of loss. Telling myself she was alive out there brought a sense of betrayal.

Feelings and thoughts ravaged my body and caused pain everywhere before I could even notice or identify them.

What do you mean you're not alone? You are alone. What do you have? A husband? Children? Friends and colleagues will leave you eventually. Stop being so naive. You ought to know better given all your education.

A rush of burning air suffocates me. Dry coughs erupt from my throat.

Why do I need a husband and children to have family? Ma, Lane is my family. She's not a friend. We have been family to each other for the last seven years. What is a family? Family is people who support you and are always there for you. Why is that family and not this? That's all those people asked. That's all they said in class. And the school showed them the door. They shooed them off like flies without a word of explanation!

A blue vein appears on my daughter's white nape. I see something light up in her and her engines begin to warm up. If we have this conversation all through the night, where will that get us? Some point of compromise that both she and I can live with? If that's a possibility, I can keep going for as long as it takes. If we can meet somewhere, I am prepared never to give up.

Ma, Lane is not a friend. To me, she's husband and wife and child. She is my family.

Husband and wife and child? You kids can't do anything. You can't get married, you can't have children – it's like you're still playing house! You are in your thirties and still playing house!

Raindrops patter on the thin windowpane.

Why can't you just accept me for who I am? I'm not asking you to agree with me on every little thing. Weren't you the one who told me that there were all kinds of people in the world? Who live different lives? You said different wasn't bad! You're the one who taught me all that. How come these things never apply to me?

Because you're my daughter! You are my child!

I want to give up. If it were an option. Cast my life as far away from my daughter's as possible. Remove myself to some place far away where I can't see her life. Throw around nice words like 'support', 'encouragement', or 'empathy' like I would with people who have nothing to do with me.

Ma. We are not playing house. That's not it at all.

Fine. Prove to me that it's not playing house. Can you be a family? Can you do anything? Can you get a marriage certificate together? Can you have children together?

It's people like you who're standing in our way. Ever thought of that?

You think it's so easy to become a family? You think it just happens overnight? What do you know about duties and responsibilities that come with it?

Ma, give us some credit. Lane and I know what that means and we know so very well how to protect ourselves. That's why we're trying our hardest.

Why are you clinging to this useless thing? Please, please come to your senses! What do I have to do? Get down on my knees and beg? Please tell me what I need to do.

If I can put my daughter back to the way she was, I am willing to do anything. I think I'll be able to do it, whatever it is. But there's nothing I can do. I can't change anything.

Ma, look at this. Look. These words here – that's me. Sexual minority. Homosexual. Lesbian. This is what I am. That's just how it is. That's what people call me, and stop me from having a family, career, everything. Is that my fault? Tell me, is that my fault?

My daughter points at the flier and says the words out loud in the end. Words I never, ever want to hear. Some words sink right into me and fall to the bottom. They pile up like a heavy, colossal breakwater, never to be moved again once they settle. Words that cannot be completely digested. Words I cannot digest. Words I cannot ever forget.

Like a cornered animal, I instinctively close my eyes.

*

All through the night, rain falls.

The wild wind raps at the window menacingly, then rushes out of the alley all at once. A long crack of dazzling light flashes on. The sound of someone coming out of the room, going into the kitchen and the bathroom. I lie in bed and listen to these sounds. Sounds raining down on me.

Everyone will point their finger at me. Mock. Even repri-
mand and punish. Who on earth do I discuss these things
with? If my husband were alive, would we be lying side by
side looking up at the ceiling and talking about this in order
to reach a wise and practical solution? No. My husband
wouldn't have had the strength to cope and might have killed
our daughter instead. As if we had never had her to begin
with. He would have chosen to pretend she never existed in
the first place.

The skies clear and morning comes once again. My daughter is already gone for the day. I look for usable scraps of cloth
in the corner of the laundry room. They're from back when
I was looking after my husband. Some of them are on a high
shelf I can't reach. On one very cold night, my husband
assembled the shelves, hammered in nails, and installed them
up there. I remember the scene vividly.

Would you like some help?

It's Lane. Before I can answer, she brings over a kitchen
chair and totters precariously up on it. Kimchi containers and
other boxes that contain who knows what are brought down
one by one. In the meantime, I stand unmoving by the laundry room doorway.

Just the cloth? Anything else?

With her hand reaching into the back of the shelf, Lane
makes eye contact with me. I scan the messy laundry room
with my eyes and finally say what I've been meaning to say.
Words tumble out without order or logic. I let the angry

words rush out of me. I let the words burn in the flames of disgust, resentment, and hate. Lane focuses on taking down the cloth and putting the kimchi containers and boxes back up on the shelf. In that moment, I want to knock the chair over and chase Lane out of this house by force, with my bare hands. I want to yank her around by the hair, tear at her face, and make sure she never comes near my daughter or this house ever again. No. I want to kill her. I want this girl, an endless source of torment, sadness, and misfortune, to disappear forever.

*

The words I spat at her follow me around all day. As I leave the house, take the bus to work, and arrive in front of the hospital, I can feel some words returning to me without fail like a boomerang. My heart trembles all the while as if I've been hit by something, or I've collided with something.

What's going on here?

The nurse on call finds me that evening in the laundry room. She looks inside the washer and makes a fuss. She pretends she happened to catch me in the act, but I'm sure the professor's wife or some other carer forgot to be discreet.

It's just some rags. I brought them from home. I'm all out of diapers.

The nurse gives me a contrived, stern look.

I understand, but this is not allowed, the nurse says. You can't do personal laundry here. This all costs extra water and detergent. It won't be fair to the other elderly patients.

I tell her that there's a bedsore on Jen's bottom. That it's mushed all over like rotten fruit and it's large enough to fit a fist. So there is no way I can reuse her diapers. The nurse stops the washer, drains it, and opens the small laundry room window about halfway.

The nurse makes herself clear: I understand, but personal use of the laundry room is strictly prohibited. There isn't a single patient here without a bedsore, and the other carers won't be happy with what you're doing.

It takes great effort to stop myself from retorting, Who cares if the carers are happy or not? I bring the half-washed cloth back to Jen's room.

Jen, who is lying wide awake in the dark acknowledges me. Mama, is it raining outside? Is it cold?

Jen calls me 'Mama' now. The first person she met in the world. I guess her mother is the only one that remains intact in her mind.

It's summer now, I say, shaking my head as I hang the pieces of cloth slippery with soap on the window to dry. It's not cold. It's not raining. It's hot. I'm sweating. I'm so annoyed I'm about to explode.

Mama, come here. Look at this. Come and look at this.

I keep my mouth shut as I take my frustration out on the cloths I'm flapping and shaking out with a snap before I hang them. Jen stirs and tries to get out of bed. I go over to her and sit her down by force. Jen tries her hardest to resist me. Her flailing arms and legs are like straws with minds of their own. And on her limbs are large, pale liver spots. Like an omen or a stigma, they are spreading all over Jen's skin.

I said sit down. Just sit, for heaven's sake.

I can't take it anymore and push Jen down on her back. She holds onto my arms and keeps herself up. I don't feel any strength or will in her grip. Jen mumbles something. The mumbles that could be pleas or curses stop and her breathing turns into violent gasps. Her face is flush and her eyes well up with tears. I quickly sit her up and pat her on the back.

I told you. I told you to sit still. Just sit still. Why are you giving me such a hard time? I need to rest, too. I'm so tired, too. I think I'm going to die. Why is everyone giving me such a hard time? Like you're ganging up on me.

Jen's breathing calms. I, on the other hand, am shaking with sobs. I try to stop, but I can't help it. Jen gently places her palm on my back. In the arms of an infirm, old woman who has nothing to look forward to but death, I weep like a child.

I'm sorry. It's my fault. It's not your fault.

When I say these words, I feel as if I'm not looking at Jen, but Jen's very imminent death. Perhaps in that way I would like to tell myself that Jen is far worse off and unhappier than me. I stop crying after a long while and catch my breath.

Because of a phone call. Jen picks up my phone and hands it to me. It's my daughter. My heart starts pounding.

Mama, Jen calls me with a terrified face when I return to the room after taking the call in the hall. My ankles ache. My lower and upper back hurts. With every move, I feel as if all the joints in my body are twisting out of place and generating pain. Or it's the things I said to my daughter coming back to claw at my heart, leave stinging wounds, and storming about inside me. I plop down on the floor by the bed. Jen pulls at my hand and puts something in it. It's a few pieces of the cloth I'd hung to dry.

Mama, there're snakes outside. Snakes. Chase them away with these.

Jen's eyes sparkle in the dark. She's lost herself again. I take the cloth, walk over to the window and hang the cloth again, saying, Shoo! Shoo!

It's there, right? The snake? Jen tries to get up and come to the window again. I say sternly to scare her, There're snakes. Lots and lots of snakes. A sense of dismay forms at my crown and trickles down my body. What to call this? I am astonished to find that these things lie in wait in all of life's nooks and crannies. Things you never want to face in life jump out at the end of some alley, just as you are turning a corner – Boo! This life is lousy with such things. Why didn't anyone warn me ahead of time?

Go away! Go far, far away! Shoo, shoo!

I lean out of the window and cry. It would be nice if

I could ward things off so simply and conveniently. If that were possible, I'd be a nice person to anyone. I wouldn't have to stand up against anything, say unpleasant things, and grope around inside me to see just how much lower I can sink. Chasing the snakes that aren't even there, or perhaps a whole nest of them writhing in the dark outside, I clench my teeth.

Early next morning, Mr Kwon summons me.

About your patient Yi Jehee, her symptoms are worsening and I think the time has come for her to move to the fourth floor where the other dementia patients are. It'll be less work for you, too, ma'am. You are getting on a bit.

A man in a suit knocks on the office door and peers in.

Could I have a look around the facilities?

Of course. Give me a second.

The family of a new patient, I gather. Mr Kwon asks the head nurse to give the man a tour, closes the door, and returns to his desk. I say that the worse the dementia, the more important it is to stay in a familiar environment. I took classes for mere weeks in order to get my carer's license, but even I know that much. Is this man under the impression that I'm doing this to kill time and make extra money? I have never worked like that in my life. Not when I was a schoolteacher before I married, not when I taught afterschool programs after my daughter was born. Putting up wallpaper, driving kindergarten vans, selling insurance, making food at a company cafeteria, I never once forgot what I was working for.

I know. I understand how you feel, ma'am. But it's not economical for us to keep that big room for just one person. The director agrees, and we're losing too much money, and anyway we're remodeling soon. Before winter.

Everyone knows how the old folks on the fourth floor are treated. They receive government assistance and they are all advanced dementia cases. Every day, patients fight tooth and nail to escape from the place – the nurses may argue that this is a common symptom of dementia – and padlocks are installed at every door to keep them locked up. How can a ward like that heal and comfort sick people?

Sitting on the edge of the sofa, I add a few words. The words are less logical reasoning than stream of consciousness. As I speak, I think of my daughter, the things she said, Lane, and Jen shaking and screaming about snakes when the sun goes down, and my husband who is dead and gone. Like Whack-a-Mole, thoughts keep popping up here and there. No matter how fast I whack them with my rubber hammer, they don't disappear or even recede. These things make me the person that I am. Moments when I am reminded of this fact return to me over and over again.

Ma'am, it's commendable that you are so caring of your patients, but if you keep getting attached, you won't be able to stay in this line of work for long. Don't you plan to stay on for a while? You need to be less of a soft touch. It's hard for us to watch you, too. Why don't you take the rest of the day off? I hear you've been sleeping at the hospital these past few nights. Go home and get some rest. Treat yourself to something delicious.

Mr Kwon rises from his desk and gets the door for me. In this way he pushes me out of the room before I can get in another word. I return to Jen's room to find her happily drinking her yogurt. I sit by her for a moment. This has been a peaceful afternoon free of incidents or accidents. But when I close my eyes, I can feel the palpable onslaught of things barreling at me. I've knocked over a small piece of wood without realizing, which knocked over the next piece, and then the next, creating a wave that there's no denying is crashing toward me.

*

I return after a few days to an empty house. *Tick, tick.* The second hand of the clock marches on and makes the silence and calm more palpable. Onward, onward without rest, what else draws closer with the passage of time? What's coming toward me, one tick at a time? Taking off my shoes by the door, I sit down and stay still for a moment. If my daughter and that girl were to move out, would this house return to the way it was? No. That ship has sailed.

I turn on the radio and throw open all the windows in the house. The red-hot heat of sunlight penetrates deep into the living room during the day. I go into the bathroom and fill the large basin with water. I add detergent, make soapy water, wet the sponge, and wipe down the sink. I wash the toilet and scrub off the water stains on the bathroom floor. A sharp and fragrant scent overflows in the bathroom. I go into my daughter's room and that girl's room, hang up their blankets in the sun and gather up the pillow cases and towels to boil. I scrub off the stains around the stove, wipe the sink faucet, and wipe the dust off the surface of the kitchen table and chairs. Lane's room looks the same – stack of books against the wall, suitcase sitting in the corner, tiny dolls standing on the dresser, clothes filling the small coat rack. Has she forgotten all about how I virtually begged her to leave this house? Why doesn't she pack up and leave even after everything I said to her? Maybe what I said had no effect on her? Or does she have no place to go? Will she move out to wherever, maybe tomorrow or the day after?

My daughter called me to ask if I'd really said all those things to her. Her voice was stripped of emotion. It was hard to tell if she was holding back her anger, or if she was too tired to get angry. In the background, I heard someone shouting, then music, and a burst of applause. She wasn't at any respectable place like the library or a lecture room, that much was clear.

If you're going to throw your life away, I want you out of my house.

I don't know how many times I've said that to my daughter. Nothing came from her end of the line. I was expecting resentment, anger, and even some abusive words, but it appears she's decided to give me the silent treatment now. She knows how strong and frightening a weapon silence can sometimes be.

I finish cleaning as evening arrives. Through the wide-open windows, I hear the everyday, nondescript sounds of neighbors' lives. Smells of something savory, something spicy. Voices that converge and part again, certain atmospheres and moods come in one way and gently waft out another. And I hear the front door opening. It gently closes. That girl must be back.

You're home. You haven't had dinner, have you? I made some sandwiches. Why don't you try some?

She changes out of her work clothes, washes her hands, and brings me sandwich slices. Colorful vegetables and white meat fill the space between two thin slices of bread. As if to give up, I go into the kitchen and return with two glasses of milk.

I can't have milk, Lane says. It gives me a stomach ache.

We sit across from each other and chew on the sandwiches like two people who've completely forgotten what happened a few days earlier. The sound of lettuce crunching and dry bread turning mushy as it mixes with other ingredients ensues. But I have trouble swallowing the food. It's the pickled pepper and the bitter spice she used. Or not. Maybe it's because she made it. Or because we're sitting together in such awkwardness. In the end, I put down the sandwich and say what I've been holding back.

Have you looked for a new place?

She quietly chews her sandwich. I tell her that it was wrong of my daughter to borrow the jeonse deposit from her without the means to pay her back. But I make it clear that this has nothing to do with me. I'm trying to convey that this is my house and that I cannot watch the two of them be together here like this.

As you know, I've already given you four months' rent in advance. Living expenses, too. Because those were your terms.

She looks up and meets my gaze for a moment. I hear lettuce crunching in her mouth.

If you suddenly tell me to leave, I don't really know what to do. Honestly, I can't afford to.

She puts down the sandwich and carefully dabs at the corners of her mouth. Then she plays with the condensation on the glass of milk.

If you don't mind, I would appreciate it if you would tell me what's bothering you.

I have a sip of milk. The animal taste is revolting. I spit it right back into the cup. Perhaps by drawing attention to myself in this way I'm trying not to lose the upper hand in this conversation.

Look here, I say after a long silence. I tell her that this is my house, not my daughter's house, and that I'm upset that my daughter, who is of marrying age, is not dating and has no intention of getting married. Words carrying a certain weight are threatening to erupt from me. But I cannot make the effort to be careful or choose my words well. A second of hesitation, and things I don't want to hear will flow out of her lips and I would do anything to keep avoiding what I know is coming.

I want my daughter to find someone decent and get married. It's not too late. Girls with far less desirable qualities get married and live comfortably. They have children, make up a family, and live fun lives. So why is my daughter standing in that hot, dirty street wasting her time on that nonsense? Do you know what it's like to be me watching her? Put yourself in my shoes. Think like a parent.

My face is hot.

I don't think you know what kind of life Green wants to live, Lane says. She said one time, Ma doesn't want to listen to me. Couldn't you hear her out just once? She's got her own idea of what she wants her life to be.

What on earth am I supposed to hear from her? The words rush up and get stuck at my throat. I'm afraid I will blurt out, It's horrifying enough watching the two of you in my house. What do you do when you are lying side by side in the dark at night? Can you play-act the pleasure that my husband gave me and I gave him? Like your parents had you, like my husband and I had our daughter, can you bear a child that is exactly half one and half the other? Do I have to say these bare naked words out loud with my own lips to shame her into a corner and get her to shut up? Is that what it takes to make her nod, see that she's taken a wrong turn somewhere down the road, and ask for forgiveness?

Look here. My daughter is not that kind of person. I know. I know my daughter.

All parents think that. But we are over thirty. We're not children.

I sweep my arm to fan myself, but accidentally knock over the glass of milk. The white milk wets the floor table and drips onto the floor.

She quickly hops to her feet, and I lose all control.

Hey, I'm not done. Sit down! Sit down and listen!

I make her sit and listen. You think you know everything? Then answer me this: Why is my daughter, who's a highly accomplished person, treated like that at work? Why is she standing out in the street every day making a spectacle of herself? If you're so smart, why don't you tell me why she's treated like that? What's bothering me? How can you ask that? What a stupid question! How stupid do you think I am? You think I'm old and don't know anything, so you can just ignore me?

Words pop out without order or logic. She leaves me yelling, goes into the kitchen, and brings back a dry rag. She calmly mops the spilled milk.

Do you think I make Green unhappy? That I'm ruining her life?

Yes. Of course. You are making my daughter unhappy. It's

all because of you. You are making me and my daughter so miserable.

I clench my jaw as hard as I can, but the corners of my eyes twitch.

She picks up the glass and puts it upright on the table. What if Green is not unhappy? she asks. Everyone has an idea of a life they want to live.

A life she wants to live? Do your parents know what you're up to? What kind of parents can come to terms with a situation like this? You think a person's life belongs to just that one person? No life is like that.

My parents struggled with it at first. Especially my father. My father is—

I wave her off to say I don't want to hear it.

I want to tell you my side of the story. If that's okay with you.

I instantly shake my head. And I say in a tone that is close to begging, Please let my daughter live a normal, ordinary life. Please leave. Please let her go. Please let my one and only child go through life without sticking out. Let her blend in and live a natural, ordinary life.

I would like you to think about why Green was standing there, Lane finally says in a firm tone. And she tells me that she's the one who pays rent and supports my daughter, and that this has been going on for over two years.

You think I'm doing this for her without any thought in my mind or any trust in her? Do you think it's possible to do something like this for someone who means nothing to me? Making money is hard work for me, too. Sometimes it's so hard I wish I were dead. You still think I have no claim to any part of her?

I want to tell her I'll pay her back. Every last bit, no matter how long it takes. But I can't bring myself to say those words.

Lane asks, If I were your daughter, what would you have said to me?

Lane says, We've been together seven years. Do you know how long seven years is? I don't understand why you still think that Green and I mean nothing to each other. Don't you think you're being too harsh?

Then she clears the plates and cups and goes into her room.

*

I get a call as I head out early next morning. It's the member of staff at the carer agency who got me the job at the nursing home. The voice of this woman who spent twenty years as a head nurse at a hospital is professional and oddly intimidating.

Ma'am, you understand I got you a nursing home position that's close to home and has good benefits, right?

I tell her I understand as I hurry along. Jen is being moved to the fourth floor this morning. I rush to work not having decided whether to say goodbye to Jen or to try harder to dissuade Mr Kwon.

So why did you go and say those things? Knowing how nursing homes are run? Mr Kwon did not sound happy.

When I come out of the alley and reach the main street, I see my bus right at the bus stop. Just then, I lose my balance and sprain my ankle. The sharp pain shoots straight up to my head and makes my hair stand on end. The agency woman keeps yapping away, oblivious to what's going on over here.

What can you do for these people who have reached the end of their lives anyway? It's sad, but you know how it is. Nothing to be done about the way of the world.

'Way of the world?' Everything that has nothing to do with her is all 'the way of the world' that she can put away in some place where she doesn't have to see it. I don't like her tone. She probably talks like that all the time wherever she goes. She's probably constantly telling her children that too. And her children will say that to their children. And in that way, things that can be labeled 'the way of the world' and put out of sight are created one after the other. And they become something large, solid, overwhelming, and terrifying that cannot be changed through the efforts of just one or two people.

She's not a severe dementia case. I'm saying she doesn't have to switch wards. That's all I said. What's there for Mr Kwon to be 'not happy' about? I say, sitting on someone else's stoop and massaging the ankle I sprained.

I can feel swelling coming on around the ankle bone. A deep-throated bark comes from inside the gate. A large dog comes dashing across the yard inside and glares at me through the crack in the front door, baying ferociously. I quickly get away from the stoop and limp away. With each step, I feel something splashing inside me, about to spill. Sense of anger and betrayal. Disappointment and resentment. A feeling that all of this is unfair. In the midst of these feelings all clumped into one, I see my daughter, that girl, and the unpleasant realities of my home.

Ma'am, if Mr Kwon says he's unsatisfied with your performance, there's nothing we can do. It'll be difficult to find you a place that's as good. Just don't say anything and go along with it, okay?

No one likes it when someone makes a sharp observation and takes it upon themselves to spell it out. I was born and raised in this culture where the polite thing to do is to turn a blind eye and keep your mouth shut, and now I've grown old in it. So why am I suddenly seeing these things as if for the first time at this point in my life? When I've already spent a lifetime going along with it and not saying a word? Why make such a big deal out of this?

I find Jen lying in her bed with her arms and legs tied down. Standing next to the grunting, twisting Jen is a burly man on a phone call. A static buzz coming from the walkie talkie on his belt informs him that the ambulance is on the way. He raises a hand and stops me from getting near Jen.

Then he gestures at her and tells me she's being transferred to another facility.

Mama? Is that you? Mama, get this off me. On the feet. It hurts. Ow.

Jen is writhing as she calls out to me. I demand to know what's going on. The man goes out into the hall and calls the nurse. The head nurse comes running and the patients and carers in the hall stop to watch.

You can't do this. You told me yesterday that she was moving to another ward, and now she's being sent to a different facility? Overnight? She may be an old woman without family who doesn't know what's going on, but this is not how you treat people.

I know what kind of place can take a patient on one day's notice: a place that pumps patients full of sedatives and gives them nothing to do besides expend all their energy waiting for death. My voice continues to rise. The head nurse pulls me aside and whispers. There's irritation and disgust in her voice as she tells me not to make a scene.

Is Mr Kwon in there? I'll talk to him myself.

He's not in. He's out on business.

Another nurse shows up. In the meantime, the man shoos away the small crowd that's gathered to watch. The scared old patients stumble back, and their carers coax them back into their rooms.

Come! Let's all take a breather, huh? Just come here for a second. The professor's wife comes out at last and stands between me and the head nurse. She sends the head nurse back to the office with some appeasing words and drags me into the stairwell.

What has got into you? This isn't your first patient! It's not like you to obsess over the old woman. She's not your family. Did she secretly promise to leave you money? Why are you getting so worked up over some old lady going to another facility?

The ache in my ankle spreads up the leg. My back hurts and the tips of my fingers tingle. I sit on the steps and press on my stinging eyes.

What is it? What's going on with you? The professor's wife presses me. I shake my head.

How do I explain that I see myself in that woman whose wrists and ankles are bound? How do I articulate such a vivid premonition? Is it her fault that she has nothing and no one? Am I seeing myself in her because I've given up hope of depending on my daughter in old age? Will I – and even my daughter – likewise find ourselves punished by a rude, wretched wait for death at the end of our interminable lives? How far will I go to avoid that?

Why is my heart always on tiptoes on the lookout for possible things to fear on the horizon?

There are people my age who still live like they're in their twenties and thirties. People who know when to butt in and when to stay out of it. People who have time on their side. People who are qualified to have that advantage. Or maybe all my behavior is that of an old woman. Trapped in this idea that I'm old, drawing strict lines between things I am or am not capable of, lopping off certain possibilities from my life, racking my brain to make the task of living as free from obstacles as possible. To hack away at the overgrown weeds and clear the path so I can look death squarely in the face as it draws near down the manicured final stretch of life. Drilling into myself that I no longer have what it takes to start over, fight, and win, maintaining a monotonous yet safe, helpless yet uneventful life.

But this is wrong. You know it is. They can't do this to her, I say as I get up, putting my weight on the wrong foot. I fall back down, clinging to the railing, and carefully get up again.

She is the way she is now, but think about the life she lived. Think about the crowds of people who brought her here and asked us to take good care of her. And when she was fine? Remember all the nice things she used to say to you? Good god! And now they're throwing her out like garbage. You think it'll be any different with us? You think we'll never find ourselves tied down to hospital beds? Do you really think that? Open your eyes. Think about it, for heaven's sake.

I might be thinking about myself, not Jen, as I say these words. I might be thinking about my daughter, not me. This isn't 'the way of the world', but my business. My business that's waiting at my doorstep. I am surprised that I had these words in me somewhere. I can hardly believe that these words that had sunk deep inside me are surfacing and coming out through my own lips rather than resting heavily all the way to my grave.

*

Outside the window, the sun is setting.

I run the tip of my tongue over the ulcer in my mouth. It keeps growing, making it difficult to put food in my mouth and swallow. All I've had all day is a few cups of lukewarm water. When I open my mouth, the empty stomach sends up an acidic stench of hunger. My vision keeps spinning and a dull light-headedness whirls around my head. I pat myself on the aching knees and massage my tight shoulders as I remind myself, Keep it together. Keep your head on straight.

Maybe I'm afraid I'll regret the mess I've made. The time I spent explaining to Mr Kwon blow by blow why Jen was not to be moved to another facility, and what I would do and how if he were to move her anyway – it was brief. But no one here is willing to think about the things I had to put on the line and the fear I had to face for that brief moment. That explains the identical hostility and derision I got from everyone.

Yes, I understand. I see how this matter may appear that way from your perspective, ma'am. But that wasn't our intention. If she moves to a facility specializing in dementia, she'll be able to receive better care. But I understand what you're saying. We will have Jen stay with us for now, and we'll talk about this again later.

Mr Kwon backed down surprisingly quickly – what's he up to? What calculations is that shrewd, cunning man doing in his head?

The restraints have left marks on Jen's wrists. The marks don't stand out against her dark skin tone, sagging flesh, and patches of liver spots. There is so much more than what catches the eye. I pull the covers over Jen's scrawny arms.

Mama, did you find my money? Jen whispers after a long silence.

I thought she was asleep, but she's blinking at me in the dark. When I don't answer, her voice grows louder. The switch in her head must have been flipped and she's lost herself again. In moments like this, I think: how ludicrous the pointless things I supposedly did for the benefit of this old woman who can't tell what's going on anyway. I reach around and pat myself on the shoulder to chase away these thoughts.

Mm-hmm. I found it. I did. It's in the drawer here.

Really? Where was it? Jen whispers.

Well, you know. The old man who draws. The one who shouts.

I knew it. Did you teach him a lesson?

I did. I gave him an earful.

Did you really find it? Can I see? Can I?

I take down the bundle wrapped in a scarf from Jen's

shelf. Commendation letters and plaques, newspaper and tissues, cans and glass bottles are gathered together.

See? I put it all in here where no one can find it. In case someone else tries to take it again. So I hid it all in here.

Jen gives a contented nod and smiles shyly, lips in a pout. If she were to turn her head and look in another direction for a moment, the conversation we just had will be wiped clean from her memory and she'll be asking me the same question again. What on earth was this woman thinking, wasting her precious youth like that? Pouring all her time and passion and money into problems in other worlds that have nothing to do with her?

That night, as I am leaving the nursing home, I get a call from Lane. I've never called, nor received a call, nor spoken on the phone with her, but I must have saved her number a long time ago. The professor's wife, who's been awkward around me all day, uses this opportunity to take off.

Aren't you going to answer? the young newcomer asks. The phone stops ringing as I fumble with it trying to decide. I look down at it, not knowing what to do, and ask, How many kids do you have?

Two. A girl and a boy, she answers. Her face is swollen after a day of tiring labor. Her hair is greasy and the handle of her bag is tattered. She opens it and sprays herself with a small bottle of cheap perfume. The smell that reminds me of cheap air freshener wafts around us and disappears.

My kids keep telling me I smell, she says.

Grade school kids?

One's in grade school and the other's still in day care.

Mm. Tough age.

The newcomer and I press close against the buildings every time cars squeeze by in the small alley. We can't avoid stepping on the trash people have thrown on the ground. I'm clutching my phone anxiously.

By the way, why did you do that today? The newcomer asks when we've almost reached the end of the alley. As I search for an answer, she adds, To tell you the truth, I was really glad you said that. I just was. I keep forgetting these things when I get caught up in trying to make a living and all, but everything you said was true.

I am about to talk about Jen, and the special, noble work she did as a young woman when the newcomer says, as if to herself, My mother's also in a nursing home. I keep telling myself I'll see her next week, or the week after that, but I just can't find the time. If I don't go and see her this month, it'll have been four months. But the truth is, whether or not the children come to check up on their parents, it's the nursing home's job to look after the parents as long as the children pay. Regardless of the life the patients lived, it's the nursing home's job to do the work they're paid to do. I don't get why they won't do even that much. Sons of bitches.

The newcomer and I part ways, and I'm looking down at the phone again when Lane calls. The second I answer, her voice jumps out at me: Where are you? Can you get over here right now?

*

It begins to rain.

Rain comes down increasingly hard. There is a crowd gathered in front of the school. The police are there, and there are also people who are not the police. I try to get closer, but I can't see the university's gate or the people blocking the gate over the crowds in front of me. Far ahead, someone holding a microphone is shouting something. It gets buried in the ambient din.

My daughter is standing somewhere over there. The same place where she was making herself heard in the scorching sun the other day. Where she gave out fliers and tried her hardest to get people to see. A place perhaps farthest from the institution you might call a school. A position in the world I had never imagined for my daughter.

It's dark and I can't gauge where that very spot was. Perhaps somewhere over there, I think to myself as I try to get another step closer. Pushing past the strong shoulders lined up side by side, I try and try to find a small gap. But none of them seems willing to let me through. Each time I raise my head, a glaring light stings my eyes. I can't tell if they're car headlights, search lights the police brought, or lighting equipment the protesters put up. The lights bounce off the transparent umbrellas and raincoats in all directions. I rub the corners of my aching eyes.

Excuse me, I mumble. Excuse me, coming through. Could you let me through?

My voice scatters in the noise of the street and the shouts of people.

Out with the unqualified lecturer! Someone shouts. The people around me shout, Out! Out! Out! People standing in a dense pack pump their fists in the air and try to press forward. Their breathing becomes rough and aggressive. I cannot see them, but I can feel them growling. The smallest spark could start a fire and set them ablaze.

I twist around and manage to reach into my bag.

Where are you? I call Lane and yell into the phone. Where are you? Just as I begin to hear her voice on the other end of the line, someone wearing large boots steps on my foot. I lose my balance and drop my phone. I quickly bend down and feel around, but I can't see it among the innumerable pairs of boot-clad feet.

The sacred place of learning is no place for homosexuals.

Hateful words inspire ever more hateful words. Firm shoulders and strong arms knock into me from all directions. Before long, I find myself surrounded by tall people in raincoats.

Green is a little injured. I'm on my way, too. But I called you just in case.

When Lane told me that over the phone earlier this

evening, should I have asked her what happened? I hear the faint sound of distant sirens as colored lights flash. People step back all at once, and a few are knocked to the ground. I focus all my attention on not stepping on the people who've fallen down. Even in my desperate attempt to find my phone.

People shout at the crowd opposite them. Curses erupt out of them as though they'd been lying in wait. Words without order or logic become entangled in the air and instantly form a large cacophony. The crowd is swept up by tense, violent feelings. No one knows what they're saying, what it means, or what they're feeling as they are carried away by a pitch-dark current of rage.

I am no exception: where am I standing, and where should I be standing? I don't know.

Rain falls hard on the top of my head, wets my hair, and drips down onto my face, the nape of my neck, and shoulders. The insides of my shoes have been sopping wet for a while now. Dragging my soaking shoes along with me, I look for any possible exit. But I'm surrounded, and there is no way I can get myself out of here.

People suddenly change direction and begin to move. Shouts erupt. Screams come from somewhere toward the university gates. I hear windows breaking and something being battered and knocked down. Wild, crazed sweep of lights. Fighting the urge to flee, I take one step, and then half a step forward. The rain comes down harder. I look up and see the sky thick with iridescent raindrops.

Things I cannot see, things I'd rather not see, flash in my mind's eye. My daughter is there. She is curled up in a ball and scared. Surrounded by people in a place where who knows what will flare up next, she's vulnerable to all kinds of danger.

Hostility and hatred, derision and abuse, rage and ruthlessness – she's right in the midst of it all.

Tightly coiled feelings that reside inside the darkest part of everyone. Feelings that lie in wait deep at the bottom, eyes gleaming. The blinding lights are carelessly resurrecting these hidden emotions.

A siren blares from behind. People are slow to make way as the ambulance shows itself. I manage to get behind the vehicle and inch forward with it. Voices calling out for people. I hear the sharp sound of girls crying in frail, high tones. But I can't get closer to these voices. Before I know it, I'm surrounded by the crowd in large boots again. Get out of the way! Load the gurney! Close the back! Shouts from the ambulance come undulating through the noise of the crowd. Who got hurt? Is it so bad they needed an ambulance? Is it my daughter? My heart starts to pound. It feels as if hot blood is traveling up the back of my neck and crawling over my head. My body is shaking from cold sweat, but my face is so hot I think it'll explode. I feel I am about to wet myself any minute now. Whimpering like a dog that needs to pee, I grab the arm of someone standing nearby.

Excuse me, could you please help me? Please take me over there.

People lean in toward me as if they're going to listen, then shake my hand off and step away.

Ma'am, you shouldn't be here. You can get out that way, a man warns me.

A car horn tears through the din of sirens. I reflexively grab the handle of this man's bag.

Excuse me, please help me get out of here. Over there. Take me to where the ambulance is. Or, actually, I really have to pee. Do you know where the bathroom is? Please, please help me. Please get me out of here.

The man looks down at me with uncertainty. I wipe the corners of my eyes and keep blinking. I have a hard time keeping my eyes open because of the heavy rain. I can't see a thing. The man says something to the person standing next to him and begins to clear some space around him by shoving the people nearby.

Hold onto this. Stay close behind me.

I want to sit my bottom down. I want to lie comfortably, wherever that may be, take a few deep breaths, and calm myself down. Go somewhere away from here and watch this scene like the evening news. That things happened in that place, I want to observe from a distance like someone who has nothing to do with it. But it's getting harder to do. The

115

people around me and a certain world keeps pushing me to the center and forces me to stand right in the middle of it.

Now, let's see what you do.

Back in the moment, perhaps everyone is staring at me with keen eyes. As I make every effort to get out of there as fast as I can, they might be giving me dirty looks as if to say, We knew it.

At a small restaurant with its lights on, I beg for permission and go into the bathroom. I push open a small wooden door right by the kitchen to see a small sink and a toilet. My wet trousers cling to my legs and I struggle to pull them down. I manage to pull my trousers down, and the second I sit on the toilet, urine pours out of me. I think it's going to gush out of me, but it quickly turns into trickles. A fart bursts out of me and I shamelessly mumble to myself, My god. My god. How on earth?

Fever claws hard at my nape and makes its way up to my face. My temples pulsate. I feel my head is about to explode any second now. A body I cannot control. A mind I cannot control. All I have left now are things I cannot control.

Are you okay?

When I come out of the store, the man who was waiting outside comes up to me. In this moment, there's nothing I dread more than questions like 'Are you okay?' Don't draw me in with such tempting bait. As soon as it's in the water, it'll take next to nothing to hook certain words, certain feelings that I can hardly cope with. I am so vulnerable that it's come to that. A chill comes over me. I shake like an animal soaked in the rain.

You're not here for the protest, are you? With no umbrella in this rain? You're sopping wet.

Could I use your phone? I have to make a call.

I feel carsick. I think if I look down, I'll instantly vomit. I take his phone. But I can't remember my daughter's number. I always called her by pressing the speed dial. I don't even know my daughter's phone number. I cannot even call her. How much else have I forgotten? I whimper in the rain with the phone in my hand.

What's all this? What on earth is going . . . going on? I don't understand. I have . . . I have never seen anything like this before. Was someone . . . someone hurt? Do – do you know? Do you know what . . . what's going on?

Something warm bathes my pupils, then is immediately mixed in with the rain. The man hesitates for a moment, and speaks. He chooses his words and sentences carefully. It is clear he is being considerate so this old woman can understand. But words that cannot be substituted or euphemized in the end fall from his lips. Unqualified. Homosexuals. Do not meet standards. Lesbian. Abnormal. Words I absolutely do not want to hear. The words throw open a door inside me that had been locked. The feelings I've been struggling to hold back come rushing out.

People like my daughter stand in the middle and on one side are her supporters, and on the other, people who oppose

117

her. The police and university staff have come out to disperse them. Where in this mess was I standing? How long was I standing there? And what about this man? But these are questions I cannot ask out loud.

My legs give out and I fall.

You can't sit here, ma'am. You need to get up.

The man quickly picks me back up by the armpits.

My knees hurt so much I think they're about to break . . . People won't get out of the way . . . I lost my phone . . . I don't know my daughter's phone number . . .

I ramble on and give up on trying to stop crying. I let myself go for a while. There's no reprieve from the rain that keeps coming down. At the far-off gate, a cry erupts.

*

Instead of going to work the next morning, I head over to the hospital where I am told my daughter has been admitted. The weather has cleared completely. It's still quite warm out, but I can tell that the summer has passed its peak and started to give way to fall.

You're here. You must have been shocked to hear.

When I step into the hospital lobby, someone comes up to me and says hello.

We met at your place that time we spent the night. Do you remember me?

I grab her hand without a thought and nod. My throat is

sore and I'm hardly able to make a sound. Each time I swallow, it's like trying to swallow thorns. I nearly burst into tears as I say my daughter's name. In the meantime, another person arrives. They exchange words in hushed voices. Their faces blur and mingle before my eyes. Someone holds my trembling hand and gently hugs my shoulders.

Don't worry. Green isn't badly hurt. She's in the Intensive Care Unit for now, but she'll be out soon.

The voice is soothing, but I can sense the anxiety and tension it holds, the fear and concern.

The Intensive Care Unit? I open my mouth and a raspy voice comes out.

Green is fine. But Yunji's condition is serious. Gyeong-yi, too. The schoolteacher, you know. And the other one works at a research center? You've probably forgotten.

I feel as if I am lifted up in the air and spun around. We walk, supporting each other, clinging to each other. Patients in hospital gowns and people pushing wheelchairs glance at us as they go by. When I finally make it to the ICU on the third floor, I see Lane getting up from the bench outside. Her cheek is swollen on one side as if she's been punched. She has a white bandage wrapped around her head and one arm in a cast.

Are you all right? I didn't know you'd lost your phone. I kept calling but you didn't answer. And things were hectic.

Her parched lip cracks right down the middle and blood seeps out. I hand her my handkerchief and plop down on the bench. Then I stare at one spot on the hallway floor. My head hurts as if a cobbler's awl has been driven through my temples. Or maybe something sharp is unfurling inside me.

Thorns. Nails.

Maybe I've been growing and harboring these things all along. I might have thought these things would protect me from the outside world, from someone. But what they do is bring me such horrific pain. I observe fearfully as the ache clouds my head. Please, please, stop. I beg, but the words only roll around in my mouth.

As people said, my daughter is fine. The moment I see her walking toward me, a heavy wall inside me topples and things that I would call light and air begin to flow through me again.

Are you okay? Are you really all right?

I finally ask after thoroughly examining and touching the tears on her forehead and elbows, and the toes missing toenails.

How badly hurt are the people in the ICU? Is it bad?

My daughter meets the eyes of the people standing around the bench and speaks with them. Then she comes back to me, holds my hand, and says, Ma.

She says that one word and is silent for a long time. She sniffles, then begins to wail. Her hair clings messily to her face, wet with tears. She's trying to say that they were badly hurt. In that moment, I am so relieved that my daughter was spared.

I use my daughter's phone to send the head nurse and the professor's wife a short text. More people come. The parents of people in the ICU also arrive. Those who were told they couldn't see their relatives yet sit near me and stare blankly at the floor. Watching them, I am ashamed that I was so relieved that my daughter was spared. Nevertheless, I'm anxious to take her home to safety.

She might end up paralysed from the waist down. Yunji.

This is the sort of thing I have to hear from my daughter when I finally bring her down to the cafeteria for a bite. She's referring to one of the two in the ICU. I don't ask her which one Yunji is. I don't want her thinking about them now.

Yes. But for now eat something, won't you? Don't speak. Just eat, I beg.

My daughter puts down the spoon and tells me what happened. She mumbles to herself through exasperated sighs, despair, and sadness.

People had fallen on the ground. And they stepped on them. Threw things at them. As the police watched. With so many people watching. Such a skinny girl. She screamed and screamed in pain. Those people. They weren't even human. Bastards.

My daughter's hand trembles like a leaf as she touches her lips. Lane, sitting next to her, wraps her arms around my daughter's shoulders.

Ma, they even . . . baseball. What do you call it? Bat. Baseball bat. I saw, I saw someone holding a bat. It was, it was night. So dark, so dark we couldn't see. There were, there were so many people. There were people like that. People

121

like that there. All people I . . . I'd never seen . . . in my . . . in my life.

Lane puts the spoon back in my daughter's hand.

Have a bite, Lane says. Let's eat first.

Just a little bit, I say. You have to eat. Eat first, and we'll talk.

She tries to eat. She picks up a few grains of rice in her soup. Tears drip from her chin onto the tray and into the soup. People who look like nurses steal glances at us. I get a spoonful of rice, push it in my mouth, chew energetically, and swallow. Like a parent teaching her child how to eat. Like I taught her long ago to chew, swallow, and made sure it was all gone – *Aah, open wide!* I try my best.

Sitting across from me, the girls eat with their heads bowed. So close I could reach out and touch them. I didn't know just how far away they were, how they were, or even where they stood with their feet planted in the ground. Everything is becoming clear now. They stand right in the middle of life. They are standing with their feet planted on firm ground, not in fantasies or daydreams. Like me. Like everyone else. They exist in the thick of life, terrifying, relentless. What they see from where they stand, what they are trying to see, what they will see, I cannot even imagine.

I cannot bring myself to swallow the rice as I try to hold in the burning things that keep gushing up.

*

How many people were gathered that day around what time and why? the reporter asks.

It was just a protest against the unfair dismissal. As usual, it was me, two other lecturers, people from NGOs, three students, and people I know, my daughter answers.

I've been told that there was an official meeting with the school administration scheduled for that morning?

There was, but it was cancelled. How do you have a meeting without the department head or the university president present? Who're you supposed to meet with? She crunches the bottled water noisily in her hand.

What you're ultimately demanding is for the lecturer in question to be reinstated, is that correct?

There's no 'reinstating' to do. That lecturer and I, we are just lecturers who get paid by the hour. We're not here to get severance or pension. The lecturer was on a one-year contract. Not even a year – nine months.

So you are not hoping to get the lecturer reinstated?

We just wanted an apology. And a promise that this would not happen again in the future. Because the university fired a lecturer for an absurd reason. I wouldn't be here if the grounds for dismissal made sense. Terrible student evaluations, for example – those are acceptable grounds for dismissal.

The reporter writes something on his tiny notepad, but I don't think he's listening closely to what my daughter's saying. A delivery guy on a scooter races in through the university gates. A startled flock of pigeons all fly up at the same time and knock over some of the pickets.

What do you make of the 'inappropriate lectures' that the university stated as grounds for dismissal? I was told that the lecturer gave a lecture that was not appropriate.

That's their justification. But it's really an excuse. Hang on. She beckons someone, and a girl with a short ponytail and a boy in round glasses go over to them.

Ask these students if the lecture was really inappropriate, she says.

While the reporter speaks with the students, my daughter steps back and holds her tongue. And I watch her from a distance. I can't tell anything for certain: what she's seeing or thinking, or how she's feeling as she stands over there. Everything is a mystery to me, and it makes me anxious and tense.

But was it really necessary to screen a film like that? For the students? the reporter turns to my daughter and asks.

Because it's part of the lesson. And we must give out assignments. The assignment was to watch the movie, discuss it, and submit a response. It was an important film that students had to see. In any case, the lecturer has the right to plan lessons. It's always been that way. For me, for all the other lecturers as well.

I thought she was looking at me, but she turns completely around to face the reporter. A hand on her hip and weight on one foot, her stance suggests she's angry.

By the way, how would you characterize your relationship with the lecturer?

A colleague.

You must be close.

Listen. You think I'm here just to defend a friend? I've given up two courses at another university to be here. That's how important this issue is to me and to other lecturers. Planning lessons is the lecturer's most basic right.

The reporter cuts her off: Do you by any chance support homosexuality?

I can't hear her answer. But I can assume what she would have said. She never hides or holds back. It's always one or the other for her. She's never stood in a gray area that's neither here or there, nor has ever tried to. She's exactly like my late husband. No, maybe this just means she's young. To be young is to be foolish. The child running around and around the picnic table humming a tune approaches me shyly. I reach out and grab the child's small, soft finger. Fluffy as freshly steamed rice. So soft it would melt like ice cream in my mouth.

It's hot, huh? Come here. Come on.

It's hot, says the child.

Does this child know that his mother is in the ICU? Does he have any idea why? Why his grandma and grandpa are standing in the sweltering sun, glaring at the world while his father keeps his mother's bedside at the hospital? What face will this boy pull when his mother, who used to pick him up with her strong arms and legs, appears before him in a wheel-chair? Even as these thoughts pass through me, I desperately try not to look in the direction of the child's grandparents. Maybe I owe this old couple an apology. Maybe I should bow before them and weep as I confess that all of this happened because I raised my daughter wrong. But how to say out loud that their precious daughter was injured because of my daughter? I cannot imagine what goes on in the minds of this couple who say it's no one's fault.

I draw the small boy to me and wipe the sweat off his forehead.

Here, you want to sit?

The boy, small as an acorn, sits next to me. I gather several sheets of fliers, fold them up and fan the boy with them. His soft, shiny locks flutter gently in the breeze. The child swings his dangling feet in the air.

The questions continue: How long have you been with your partner? The person you are living with now?

Seven years, my daughter says, tension momentarily lifting from her face. She must be thinking of Lane and what she will be doing now. Sautéing, roasting, frying by the hot stove.

But where's the hope in such a relationship? Won't it be over when they break up?

Now I am the one asking questions. I am thinking of the details that make up this thing people call love, this meaning-less, hollow word, 'love'.

For instance, when you lie in bed together at night and

caress each other, what can you do, and how? Can you even call that sex? Can you enjoy the pleasures or joys a woman can feel? If yes, how?

These primal curiosities. Questions no different from everyone else's. That child who sprang from my own flesh and blood is perhaps the creature I'm most distant from. One I have never managed to make sense of. I want to ask her if that's really truly what she wants. A relationship that cannot make a child. A meaningless bond that cannot create anything. A life that will remain incomplete to the end. And the subsequent loathing and insults that will follow them relentlessly like shadows. The weight of humiliation and self-blame they will have to bear.

Is that really what you want?

I want to know. Just as that person who's got nothing to do with her does. Holding a small notepad and pretending to take notes sometimes. With no expectation, agenda, or fear, I want to ask anything and wait for the answer. But how frightening it is to become aware of things.

Nevertheless, I must ask. I have to. I must be prepared to ask and ask until I tire myself out. Because my daughter is my child. In the end, I want to know, and I must know. I don't want to be the kind of parent who runs away. I don't want to avoid and hesitate, and end up losing my daughter.

But this school was established by a religious foundation. So it would appear that this is a difficult issue for them to understand. Any thoughts?

The reporter is shielding his eyes from the sun. I cannot see what expression he's wearing.

There is nothing to understand. And it's not an issue that requires understanding in the first place. This is just a basic right. Something that everyone is born with. And professional life is separate from private life. Is what I'm asking for such a big deal? Separation of the professional and the private. Granting lecturers basic rights. This is such a given.

My daughter's firm voice carries over to me.

*

My daughter almost died.

If Jen asks, I plan to say that to her.

Why? What's going on? If Jen whispers back, I plan to chat with her all night about all the things I haven't been able to share with anyone. But when I go to work at the nursing home for the first time in three days, Jen isn't there anymore.

All they say is that she was moved to a facility specializing in dementia. Her room is empty and the wallpaper and paint have been stripped. There's a No Entry sign suggesting that they're about to start construction. The room is filled with the wet, nauseating smell of cement.

Don't say a word. Keep your head down. That's just how it is. Don't talk back, you hear me? The professor's wife, who's quick to size up any situation, hurries over and gives my hand a tight squeeze and walks away.

I'm suddenly a carer wandering the hall without a patient to look after. No one tells me what's happening to me. No one tells me what I'll be doing, how, or how much work I'll be getting from now on.

Have a seat. Mr Kwon will be right with you.

The nurses all behave awkwardly around me. As I did on the first day I came here, I sit on the squat sofa facing the reception and wait for Mr Kwon to call me into the office. He shows up long past the end of the lunch hour. He trails in behind the old nursing home director and his wife.

Oh, you're here. I heard you had something you needed to take care of. How did it go? he says.

The director and his wife go into his office, and he takes me to the dispensary.

May I see you in here for a moment? he says.

When I walk in, he slams the door shut. Outside the small dispensary window, I see two ambulances. The doors left open, long legs extend out of the driver's seat, and white smoke rising from it. The ambulance drivers must have been given a little kickback to cooperate with patient recruitment. Everyone knows that the association fee the carers are half-forced to pay is used by these facilities for bribes, offered to the ambulance drivers. They will do what it takes to find potential patients. They'll round up perfectly fine people and turn them into patients. And the patients will bring in money.

We weren't able to give her the specialized care she

required, so we found her another facility. I thought I should tell you this in person.

I don't ask why this was decided in my absence. I know how these people think. I know they'll keep the truth hidden to the very end. The car doors close and the two ambulances pull out of the parking lot.

When did she leave? I ask.

This morning, he says. They recommended that she arrive when it's still bright so she could have a meal and get a tour of the place.

I am at a loss for a moment as I look at the small syringes, long nozzles, boxes of antiseptics, and large barrels of pills filling the shelves of the dispensary.

These words suddenly pop out: Are your parents living, Mr Kwon?

If they are, they must be well over eighty. I'm not hoping to alter anything with these words. He quickly picks up on what I'm trying to say.

They passed away, he says. Long time ago.

So he might be lying.

Could they have done something like that to their parents? Those people? I mutter and cannot help but add: This is not right. Without asking anyone for consent. Without a word to me. This is really not okay.

If she had family, we would have asked for their consent. But as you know, that is not the case. Legally, we are not required to ask the patient's carer for consent.

Mr Kwon looks irritated and exhausted. It's not fair to judge this one person by a strict moral standard and ask him to take responsibility. I know that. The activity we call work these days is ruined and depraved. It has been a long time since it lost the ability to imbue a person with a sense of fulfillment and pride as it did to for our generation. People are no longer masters of their work, but slaves that must stay on their toes in order not to be pushed out and ignored. And the time finally comes when one is ejected from the world of work and must admit failure.

We'll give you until the end of the month to wrap things up here, ma'am.

The moment those words come out of Mr Kwon's mouth, I notice that I've been bracing myself for this moment all along. Things that don't come as a surprise but that one cannot prepare for or prevent. I ask where Jen is.

You know very well that the information is available to family only.

I was like a family to her. You know that, I say.

That's not the same, he says. He tries to say something, shakes his head, and leaves the dispensary.

I come out of the room and go over to the garbage dump at the back of the building. I open and check the filthy plastic bags one by one with my bare hands. I pick through the tissue and diapers with shit and vomit, blood and pus, and the wet newspapers, broken glass bottles, and dirty nozzles and syringes as well.

The professor's wife hurries out and runs over. What's going on? What happened? What did Mr Kwon say?

I upend the large trash bag that comes up to my waist and shake out all its contents. They make a big crash as they fall on the ground.

What on earth are you doing? The professor's wife pulls my arm. Did you lose your marbles? Stop that!

I shake her off and say, Go mind your own business.

How am I supposed to mind my own business when you're in this state? she says. What's going on? Just tell me what's going on.

I squat by the heap of trash and pick through it as I say, Why didn't you ask sooner? Why didn't you ask what was going on when they were moving her? Why didn't you give me a call?

Oh, for heaven's sake! Are you such a fool that you don't see our position here?

I manage not to ask, Shouldn't you have done something about it anyway? It's not my fault. It's not your fault. It's no one's fault. If we keep telling ourselves that, then who should all the victims of the world go to for their apology?

I am no exception, even as these thoughts run through my head. The professor's wife mutters to herself and goes back in. She might tell the newcomer and the nurses that the old crone finally lost her mind. She may whisper much worse things about me, but there's nothing to be done now. Holding myself back from doing the things I really must do just to spare myself the petty insults and rumors – that ends now. I've repeated this pattern so many times over the course of my life, and I don't want to do it again.

Finally, I find the two pieces of torn, dirty letters of commendation. Luckily, I also find the small plaque. The tip of it is broken. These were all things Jen treasured. I wipe them down quickly with a piece of tissue and put them in my bag.

*

That evening, before the sun sets, I hear the front gate opening and Lane comes back. I lie curled up on the sofa and watch her take off her shoes and come in. The blue bruise on her left temple is still there. Dried pus clings on in one corner of her mouth.

I'm sorry. I didn't know you were home.

I don't say anything back and close my eyes. The last days of summer blast a muggy heat that has me fettered and won't let go. When I close my eyes, I can feel moisture seeping in from somewhere and I grow heavier and heavier with water. I feel like the strips of wallpaper have turned soft and are coming off the walls, whose foundations are sinking, and the whole house is creaking as if ready to collapse at any minute.

A hand on my forehead.

Are you okay? Lane asks. I don't have the energy left to push her hand away.

You have a fever. Do you need to go to the hospital?

I wave her off to say I'm fine. She brings over a bean paste soup with zucchini and a bowl of thin rice porridge.

Try to eat something. I'll run out to the pharmacy for some medicine.

Lane leaves. *Tick, tick.* The long rays of the last of the day's light pour into the living room, the sound of the clock gently ringing. I slowly sit up. Bones knock into each other and awaken the pain. My arms ache as if they're being torn off. I pick up the spoon and slowly taste the food she made. I must get my strength back. I must get up. Each time I tell myself that, I think of my daughter.

My daughter is standing in the street right now.

She's standing in the street where things come and go without warning. Things I, the person I am now, cannot begin to foresee. She stands out there not knowing what's flying down the street aimed at her from all directions. When I think about that, I cannot swallow a bite. I cannot bring myself to do it.

Lane comes back. She has bought cold medicine, a bottle of medicinal herbal tea, and two packets of large muscle relaxant patches. I take the medicine and put the patches on her back and shoulders. The silent living room fills with the sound of opening the packets, taking out the patches, and crumpling plastic covers. She pulls her shirt up, and I see a long, red mark along her back and waist. Looks as if she was scratched by something sharp.

Have you had this looked at? I ask.

No. It's not that serious, she says.

The patch with the plastic cover peeled off sticks together. The cool smell of menthol rises up.

You should get an X-ray, I mutter as I separate the corners of the patch with my fingernail. You never know. It'll leave a scar. You might develop nerve pains later. That doesn't heal easily.

There is faint scarring on her back that looks like goose-bumps. There are patches where her skin has turned dark.

I had eczema. When I was young. That's all, she says.

Eczema? It must have been hard on your parents. Children have soft skin that's easily infected and scarred.

I get the patch unstuck and put it on her back. Then I pull out another and peel off the plastic. I move, and she leans to the side. A clear, black bruise on one shoulder, and a fresh red scab where the skin tore.

You should go to the hospital. You can't tell just by look-ing at it. Is there an orthopedic clinic near where you work? You should make the time to go.

Lane doesn't say a word. In the absence of answers and responses, I ask questions, answer them myself, and keep going on and on. Maybe this is how I keep myself from saying what I really want to say.

After sunset, Lane and I arrive in the street where my daughter is standing.

People who will hold the pickets overnight are there. Under the small instrument giving out light, expressions undulate over people's faces and the person at the front is saying something. I settle down at the back of the crowd, far away. Lane goes up to the front and stands side by side with my daughter. Leaning toward each other, they seem to be talking. Someone shouts something on the other side and music starts to blare. The somber atmosphere is disturbed and a momentary distraction created.

Those people have been at it for so long, I'm not even surprised. Pray for the people in the hospital, says a woman standing next to me. She's a member of the family of someone who was badly hurt last time. The one who's still in the ICU. The name that the people gathered mention with respect. Her parents are not there anymore. I don't see her young son, either. Then is this person her sister? Aunt? Maybe they're not her family at all.

Would you like some of this?

I wait for the woman next to me to finish, and offer her some fruit and a cold bottle of water I brought from home.

I see my daughter off in the distance saying something into the microphone. Her voice travels through the speakers in an even, sober tone. I cannot hear what she is saying because of the music and shouts coming from the other side. I sit, watching all the chaos around me, speechless.

The fact that I am at a place like this. The reality of being exactly where the curses and slander are being aimed. All of it feels unreal. I think I've been sucked into this ridiculous nonsense that my daughter and that girl made up, and I've been fooled again. But if this really is nonsense, how to make sense of the unquestionably tragic state of that person in the hospital who may never walk again? How to defeat the countless tragedies lurking around my daughter even at this very moment, waiting for the right moment to pounce?

So I cannot talk like the people standing on the other side anymore. I mustn't. I cannot tell these kids to stay hidden, order them to keep silent, go through life as inconspicuously as the dead, or just go and die. I cannot stand on the side with people who say such things. But this realization doesn't mean I understand these kids perfectly. So then, where do I stand? Where should I stand?

I feel for these kids. I feel sad and sorry for them. In that sense, I am no different from the many passers-by over there who stop for a moment out of curiosity and continue on their way.

Have you eaten anything?

I am able to have a short conversation with my daughter after a while.

I had dinner with the others. What are you doing here? I heard you were sick. Go home. Don't you have to work tomorrow? I'm okay. Just go.

I will.

Come home with me. The words rise up to my throat. But I don't say them out loud. If I say them out loud, I have no doubt that other words, and more words after that, will follow. I tell her I'll be heading home soon, and settle down again in a spot where I can see my daughter.

It is past ten at night. The growling of people on the other side grows quiet. They must have gone home with the resolve to return tomorrow. A long fight. A fight that prepares for a tomorrow far, so far in the future that they cannot see it from where they are now. The swarm of buses that has been roaring by all day thins out, as do the lines waiting for the buses. The stately buildings on the other side of the gates are lit up brightly like glaring eyes.

My younger sister didn't just fall out of the sky one day. She's not a monster that appeared out of nowhere. She has parents, siblings, and friends. She has people who love her.

At the front of the table, someone begins to speak in a hushed tone.

Right. That's right, I say to myself as I listen in.

We are just here. We just are. We just want to be acknowledged, like, *Yes, we see that you are here.* That's all we are asking for, another voice adds.

Yes. That's how it is, I say to myself.

I listen to the second person's story too. I listen, listen, and listen again. How much listening do I have to do before I can begin to speak up?

I am heartbroken about the discrimination against my daughter. She's gone to school for a long time and knows a great deal, but what if she gets fired from her work, becomes a slave to making ends meet, falls into poverty, and must go on doing exhausting physical labor into old age like I do? I am afraid of that happening to her. And that has nothing to do with my daughter liking women. I am not begging you to understand these kids. Only that you let them do the work they are good at and compensate them for it. That is all I'm asking for.

Something like that. Will the time come when I will be able to say these things out loud? When the fear and disappointment, betrayal and anger, and all other emotions surrounding my daughter have ebbed away? Will I be able to say that the very spot where these kids stand is at the center of a heartless world?

The next morning, I take the first bus home and my phone rings as I walk through the door.

Ma'am, is that you? It takes me forever to recognize the voice. It's the young newcomer from the nursing home.

Do you have a pen and paper? Write this down. Quickly.

She reads an address to me and I write it down on one corner of the flier.

*

Jen's new nursing home is three hours away by bus. The cab drops me off at the end of a two-lane street surrounded by endless greenhouses. Sweat pours as I make my way toward the church building far ahead. A renovated old church, the nursing home looks run down and underequipped even from this distance. Two dogs on a leash in the yard bare their fangs and bark at me.

I say to Jen, You know, my daughter almost died.

Mm. You have a daughter?

Yes. I have a daughter.

One daughter?

Yes. One daughter.

Mm. She must be pretty. Just like her mom. Can't imagine how pretty she must be if she takes after her mother.

No. The Jen I find waiting is not the kind, warm Jen I know. Jen's carer tells me that she took a turn for the worse in the last few days. Maybe they prescribed her too much sleep medication. The frail elderly patients' conditions can become irreversibly worse overnight. I listen to the carer's explanation with a blank face.

Jen lies in bed, eyes open toward the ceiling but unseeing. All I can sense is that the world she's looking at is not the world I stand in.

Jen.

I wrap my hands around hers and bring my ear close to her lips. I'd like to hear any sign of breathing, however faint or shallow. I become desperate to find signs on life in her. I run my hand across her forehead and squeeze Jen's scrawny feet under the covers as hard as I can.

She wasn't this bad last time I saw her. She was tuning in and out, but she ate okay and talked okay. Jen? Jen? It's me. Do you remember me? Look over here. Look at me.

Eight beds placed side by side in a small room. Apart from two people who are sitting up, the rest are lying on their backs, motionless. The old fan creaks each time it rotates. Apart from that sound, this place is devoid of anything that could be called sound. Or maybe something's happened to my ears. Or all my senses have pressed pause all at the same time.

I would have given her special attention if I had had the time, the carer follows me in and mutters, disgruntled. But as you know, I didn't have a moment to spare. This place is run on two twelve-hour shifts. And that day, the night shift person happened to be late.

The carer smells like sweat and wet laundry. I remember to offer her a bottle of drink that I brought with me. I offer the two elderly patients drinks as well, and have a sip myself. It catches in my throat and I explode into a fit of coughs. I try to approach this from a different angle. I mean to say, Jen does not deserve to be treated this way. She has earned the right to care with much more affection. But the words don't come out as tactfully as I'd like. I try to explain to her what kind of person Jen is.

Earned it? The carer cuts me off. So then are you saying that there are people here who deserve to be treated badly? I don't know what kind of life this woman led. There's no need for me to know the details of my patients' lives, either. What difference would that make? She would have died without anyone knowing in a place like this anyway.

The carer gets up to leave.

Did she mention anything else? I ask. Did she ask for anyone? Anyone she wanted to see? Anything she wanted to eat?

I wipe my face with a handkerchief as I ask. I'm sweating. My face keeps getting wet. One elderly man, cradling one arm with the other, limps along and looks into the room from the hall. He's looking ahead, but his unfocused eyes look right past me.

You're out of bed again? I told you to lie down! Sir! Sir!

Wait, wait a minute. I stammer, trying to tell her something.

The carer puts down the empty bottle and looks me straight in the eye. A noble life? she says. Well-respected career? Only people who think that life is very short throw around words like that. Look around you. Life is disgracefully long. And we all end up the same way: waiting for the day we finally die. Go and talk to the office staff.

At the office, all I hear is that no one can take Jen out except family. No one except direct blood relations qualifies or has rights, is all I hear. I am all but pushed out of the office and standing in the middle of the yard where the dogs are barking around me. The dogs are growling viciously, ready to attack. The enraged sound threatens to come at me and bite my ears off.

Jen will die here.

One day, curled up on her side facing the entrance, she

will breathe her last breath. The nursing home staff will remove her body, wipe down the bed and put on new sheets, and get a new patient. Jen's stiff body will be thrown in the furnace on the grounds that she has no relations. A number tag will be placed on her white ashes and stuck in a storage space for unclaimed ashes. She will spend ten years in there taking up as much space as her urn does. And then she'll be dumped in a barren field. Without a past, without memories, no will, no last words to impart, no eulogy.

Jen's death will become a cautionary tale.

I pace the yard like someone with nothing to do. The vicious dogs calm down and I squat in one corner. The sun starts to sink over my head.

I should go to Jen. I should do something.

And yet all I do is sit there helplessly and look up at the setting sun.

The damned heat. This heat is drying everyone to death.

When I glare up at the sky, my face instantly becomes soaked with sweat. I blow my nose into a handkerchief, dab the corners of my eyes, and take a deep breath. I have not given up hope yet. I'm not going to give up by telling myself, It won't work anyway. There's no chance. It's not something I can do. That's too easy. Anyone can give up. I'm not going home like this. I can't.

A small refrigerated truck putters up along the narrow, dusky road and pulls into the yard. The driver unloads ice boxes of different sizes and groceries by the entrance, hands the office staff a handwritten receipt, and says something. In the meantime, two women in aprons come out and carry the large tub of spice and groceries inside. It's as if I'm not there. No one minds me.

What should I do, and how?

The only thing that comes to mind is to push people out of the way, burst into Jen's room, and escape with her on my back. Unrealistic. A plan that won't work for me. Something that it never occurred to me to try. When I close my eyes, the sound of time being washed away down the river gives me the chills. Night and day switch places instantly, summers and winters pass, rain falls, skies clear, the trees grow thick with leaves, then give way to a tableau of bony, withered branches. Maybe I've grown irreversibly old in this season.

But as these thoughts pass through me, I do not leave. All I do is hush the voice inside me that says, Time to go home. Delay defeat. Wait. I finally get up and march into the building.

Wait a second. What did you say your relationship was? Hello? What's your relationship?

As I march to Jen's room, someone rushes out of the office and yells after me. It's the male member of staff who put his foot down and said absolutely no checking out of the facility except with family.

No relation! I'm not related to her in any way. I answer. And then add angrily, I'm just going to have her over for a few days. What's your big problem? Do you want to come in here and see the state she's in? She's just as good as dead. You think she'll live for another thousand, ten thousand years? She's about to go any day now, so who cares about procedures and policies?

The man stops short on his way back into the office.

Please, just let me have her for a few days. Just three. Or two. Or one. Please. There's really no time left. There won't be a next time.

He looks at me at a loss.

She has no family, I say. She has no blood relations. There isn't a single person under heaven who will come to see her. Family or not, what does it matter?

Surprisingly, I don't shed a single tear.

*

I promised the male staff member two days, but I have no intention of keeping that promise. But I'm not ready to take care of Jen indefinitely, either. How nice it would be if every eventuality in life held off until I'd braced and prepared myself for it. Gave me enough time to think it over and come to a decision.

I wait for morning by Jen's bedside. I'm waiting for the medication in Jen's system to wear off. I'm making sure the carers don't inject Jen with sedatives and tranquilizers. The lights go out at nine and the carers retreat into their sleeping quarters by ten. It feels as if the wards are trapped in a very solid silence. I am surrounded by a darkness so strong it won't open or break no matter how hard one strikes on the outside.

Jen, do you want anything to eat? My daughter is coming in the morning. I told her to come. You always wanted to see her.

I chatter on to keep the silence at bay. This place is so utterly dark that it's only when I'm talking that I can believe I am alive. It's as if everything has stopped. I flip the phone open and keep checking to make sure time is passing. Then I keep nodding off and waking up again.

When I finally wake up properly, I hear birds. Half-awake, I go to the window. The blue-gray light of morning lifts and the view outside becomes clear. Bright light is pouring in through the window before long. My daughter arrives a long while after daybreak. Actually, no. The back door of the cab opens and Lane steps out.

I came instead. I kept trying, but Green just couldn't get up.

While she stands off in the corner, I sit Jen up and put on the clothes Lane brought. A pink T-shirt with a bunny rabbit on it, and baggy shorts. Why did she pick out such a ridiculous outfit out of all the clothes in the house? I try not to look disapproving. Lane rubs her eyes as she gazes around the ward in bewilderment.

Jen and I sit in the back and Lane sits in the front. The taxi picks up speed as it travels down the road with little traffic. I ask the driver to turn the air conditioner down and focus all my nerves on keeping Jen comfortable. Through the side mirror, I catch glimpses of Lane yawning. I look again, and she's sleeping with her head against the window at an awkward angle, mouth hanging open. I reach down for the lever and recline her seat back a little.

Are you okay? Any discomfort anywhere? Are you hungry? What would you like to eat? Hmm? Hang in there just a little longer. We're almost there.

Sleep overwhelms me. I keep talking so as to not fall asleep. Jen sometimes turns toward me and makes eye contact as if her mind is back, but then turns blank again. And before long, I fall asleep with my mouth hanging open just like Lane.

The taxi pulls up at our front gate. Lane gets out first and opens the gate. The gate swings and bangs into the wall. I open the back door and carefully help Jen out of the car. I see Jen's face slowly become clearer, like someone waking up from a very deep sleep.

Ma, is that you? Who's that? What's going on? Huh? my daughter comes out to the gate and asks in a loud voice. I gesture at her to stop, but she doesn't. In the end, I hear sounds coming from inside the gate across the alley, and someone comes out. It's the man holding a broom.

Just getting back from somewhere?

At this moment when everyone who lives in my house is standing out in the alley, a moment I had hoped would never,

ever come to pass, when all is undeniably laid bare – I run into the man across the alley.

Yes, we're coming back from the hospital.

Jen's stooped figure struggles out of the cab. I tell my daughter to help Jen into the house, pay the driver, and shut the door. The cab backs precariously out of the alley, trying not to scratch the parked cars.

She must be your mother.

As I am about to step into the gate with the bags I brought from the nursing home, the man cannot contain himself and asks that question.

I think about just nodding, but I say, No. My mother passed away a long time ago. This lady is someone I used to take care of at the nursing home.

And then I nod, close the gate, and go into the house.

Who is she? Ma, who is she?

Unlike my daughter who keeps asking, Lane does not ask a single question. She only lays Jen down on the sofa, sits by her and gazes down at her. The children on the second floor are stomping their feet and singing. It must be time for them to go to kindergarten.

I look up at the clock and whisper, She's someone I used to take care of at the nursing home. She'll be staying with us because of circumstances.

What circumstances? Can you just bring home someone from the facility? Can you?

My daughter follows me around the house and asks me all

sorts of questions. She still has the red mark on her forehead from that day. I say it's just for a few days. And peek over at the living room where Jen is. Outside the open window is a scene so clear and bright. It feels as if we finally got through the summer and began autumn overnight.

Me and my daughter. Jen, whom I brought, and Lane, whom my daughter brought. In the house where the four of us are staying, a cool breeze flows in. All I do all day is sit by Jen and wait for evening to arrive. A calm evening comes, and like a fantasy, a day goes by without anything happening.

The morning after I go down to the district office to apply for unemployment, I open all the windows around the house and gently get Jen up. Lane, who had been looking after Jen, takes a few steps back.

Pretty. So pretty. Pretty like her mama.

Jen's soft, warm eyes land on Lane. Lane tries to say something, but I stop her.

Are you hungry? I ask Jen. Would you like to eat something?

What are we having? I am amazed to see Jen's eyes looking right at me. In these moments, she's not an old, sickly patient loitering near death with all her memories gone, but a person who's bravely made the long trek of life.

What would you like to eat? I ask, checking inside Jen's baggy pajama bottoms. Changing her diapers often doesn't do much about the smell. The nauseating smell of urine and rotting is already starting to waft around the house. I was expecting this. I was prepared for this. For the remainder of Jen's stay here, how many more unexpected things for which I am unprepared will happen?

Shall I make you something? Lane swiftly gets to her feet and asks. Jen extends her hand toward Lane, and Lane grasps it with a gentle smile spreading across her face.

*

I spend all day by Jen's side.

Thanks to that, I sometimes forget to worry about my daughter, to complain about Lane, and to bemoan my current state. My daughter disapproved for a few days before shutting up about it altogether. She probably doesn't have the luxury of caring. So it's always Lane who's helping out with Jen. When I'm out running errands, when I'm preparing Jen's meal, or giving Jen a bath, I need Lane's help. Lane's the one who takes out the heavy bag of trash filled with dirty diapers.

Grandma. Raise your arm. Like this. That's right.

Say, ah! Bigger. Aah! Aah!

Make a fist and open it again. No, not like that.

Sometimes, I think Jen prefers Lane to me. She throws tantrums and refuses to listen to me, but when Lane asks, Jen is a perfect lamb. Maybe it's because Jen is growing weaker. When I think back to Jen when we were at the nursing home, I can say for certain that her condition is getting worse.

Not all days are so easy and pleasant to get through. I sometimes fight the urge to snap and scold. For instance, when Jen knocks over a cup on the table for no reason or starts to shout, I want to go home! Sometimes she tries to escape from the bathroom with suds all over her, or pulls my hair until I howl. At times like this, I think I'm an idiot for bringing home a person I can't handle. I still manage to get through these moments, and the moments after that, with great difficulty, only just barely.

The work it takes to care for someone. The grueling task of picking up after someone else. Maybe I want my daughter and Lane to see the gruesome, punishing realities of this task that sounds beautiful and noble. Maybe I want them to experience it first-hand rather than reading about it or hearing about it.

I'm not hoping that they will look after me like this ten, twenty years from now. I want them to think about their old age, the phase one cannot imagine at all in one's younger days but inevitably comes with time. Just reflect on it, just once. And go find themselves a real partner now – someone who will share the responsibility and trust. So that when I depart, I don't leave with worries and concerns, regrets and disappointments.

Jen. That girl is not my daughter.

In the middle of the night, I lie next to Jen and whisper. I hear my daughter come home, Lane come out of the room to greet her, the light switch on in the kitchen and glassware clink, then the door to their room close and silence set in again.

My daughter brought her home. Those girls are not friends.

But that is always as far as I get. Words I cannot get out, words that won't take the shape of words and come out. They remain inside me, rattle around, knock into things, and leave wounds I feel so keenly.

What would you have said, Jen? What would you have done?

On the other hand, when I say these things, I feel as if I am consoled. At times like this, I see that I am standing in the middle of it all, not far, far away. And I know that I haven't caved in or fallen down.

*

Is someone at the door? Outside? Jen calls me one afternoon.

I come out in the middle of doing laundry and turn down the radio. Jen is beaming as she sits leaning deep in the sofa, looking up at me. I take off my rubber gloves and dust the crumbs of hodu-gwaja cake off Jen's face. There is only a handful left in the bowl that was full.

She won't be home for another hour. We have to wait a little.

I point at Lane's room. I have to open her door, open the

living room windows, and show her the empty yard for Jen to finally stop asking. But then she forgets and asks again.

Is someone at the door? Outside? Where did they come from?

I sit on the raised threshold of the bathroom washing rags and give her a half-hearted answer. It's not so much an answer as a signal that I'm here. My answers grow shorter until they turn into mumbles: Mm-hmm. Mm-hmm.

Jen keeps saying something, and I think to myself, If I'd left her at the filthy nursing home, she would have died already. It's a good thing that she's got this much better. How could they treat someone so perfectly fine like a living corpse? But what if a month passes, and then another in this way? What if my unemployment pension runs out and the time comes for me to go to work again? Do I have to go looking for a nursing home for Jen again? Will I have to?

She said children in yellow were standing around the door. Little kids like kindergarteners.

One afternoon exactly two weeks later, I'm told what Jen was saying that day. Lane tells me the story with no expression on her face. She seems to be frozen in the moment when she came running out into the yard shouting, Grandma isn't moving. A puzzled look. The face of someone who's unsure of what to do next. As I listen, my daughter wraps her arms around my shoulders.

Like little yellow chicks. She said she couldn't sleep because of the sound of little chatterbox children milling by the door. She wanted to know why they were being so loud. She asked what was going on.

Jen passed away one Saturday afternoon. Like the weather forecaster said on the morning news, it was a sunny day with a gentle breeze. My daughter went out to buy a cake, I was hanging up the laundry in the yard, and Jen had sunk back into the sofa and fallen asleep. Lane, who was washing fruit in the kitchen, thought she was asleep.

A round cake decorated with green grapes and strawberries. The cake my daughter brought home was so lovely and looked so delicious that my mouth watered just looking at it. I put the cake in front of Jen. And the plums and peaches Lane had washed next to it. And I remember thinking that I should start looking into places where Jen could go. Before the end of this month. Before the end of this season, I should find her a good place, I remember promising myself. Because I can't keep looking after Jen like this. I will be good to her for as long as she's here, I remember my resolve.

My daughter, Lane and I make our way around the small kitchen. Quiet but quick movements. I'm completely focused on Jen. So I seem to have forgotten all about the fact that Lane and I are inhabiting the same space, and the unpleasantness and awkwardness it brings. Moments without any friction, so utterly natural and calm, pass like a dream.

*

The peace Jen brought. A brief ceasefire.

And that turned out to be Jen's final gift to us. Lane stammered that she didn't realize anything had happened until she finished preparing dinner and tried to get Jen up. In the brief second when I was in the yard calling the woman on the second floor. When the phone rang and my daughter was speaking with someone. Lane held Jen's hand, stroked her cheek, and held her ear to Jen's lips.

*

Jen tastes the cake.

Just a tiny bite, which she savors and swallows slowly, then nods. Enchanted by the soft, sweet cake. A satisfied look. I add a big dollop of cream to a piece of strawberry and hand it to Jen. Just an average day for some people. Little, ordinary moments everyone has the right to enjoy.

Do you like it? I had to go really, really far to get it, my daughter says.

Maybe we could make it at home next time, Lane says. Maybe flatter like a tart.

You can do it without an oven? my daughter asks.

Jen looks back and forth between my daughter, Lane, and me.

A perfect afternoon.

*

But the moment I imagined never comes. These moments always come too soon or too late. They pass before you notice, or you give up waiting for them. The last thing Jen saw wasn't a lovely, delicious cake, but twittering little children.

The thing you see right before death.

Jen saw tender, innocent children, so she must be on her way to a better place. And on the other hand I worry that she may have noticed how I was secretly worrying about her being a burden. The two thoughts mingle. Guilt and shame rise to the surface and I feel as if all of this is my fault.

I shouldn't have thought that. I mumble to myself, rubbing my hands. Why did I have to think that?

*

Moments later, the doctor comes out of the emergency room and calls for me. With me, Lane, and my daughter watching, the doctor states the date and time of death in a clear voice, and takes off all the lines and equipment on Jen's body. Then he turns Jen on her side and asks, Are you sure you want to watch? Will you be okay?

They are going to drain the waste out of the dead body. Because she is now a dead person. They want to get through the procedures quickly. I turn and get out of there.

My daughter holds my hand. A cry slips out of me. With my daughter's arms around me, but with my eyes still looking in the direction of Jen's bed, I cry like a child. Countless emotions crash into me as they come and go – I don't think I'll ever get to explain them all to my daughter.

*

Several days go by.

The space we managed to get at a funeral facility on the outskirts is relatively small and hidden away in a corner. A member of staff follows us to the room, turns on the lights, and takes the tarp off the altar. It smells like something musty and of wet mold. Even with all the lights on, the room still seems dim.

It's just one day, I tell myself, but it doesn't make me feel better. Why did they give us this dank room out of all the empty rooms?

You never know when you'll suddenly have visitors. That's all the funeral facility employee tells us.

A life that costs money even in death. These things don't surprise me much anymore. It's one of those things you see frequently everywhere. I look up at the grimy corners of the ceiling and through the gap in the warped door. Two people in overalls bring two large flower pots. The incense burner is set up, and the incense is lit. The sharp scent of it fills the room.

What about the funerary portrait?

I pull out a picture that I am sure was cut out of an old

magazine. The picture is so small it hardly fills half the frame. A funerary plaque bearing Jen's name is placed on the altar, and above, her picture. The altar still looks empty.

She was stylish, my daughter says as she looks into the picture frame.

These glasses are popular nowadays. Pretty, huh?

Yeah.

My daughter asks, Lane answers, and they chat in whispers.

Do you have a sangju? The employee comes by with the itemized list of expenses and asks if we've picked a sangju, or chief mourner. I tell him we won't be getting many visitors.

You will have to have a sangju. We have to put up the name, and we keep a record here as well.

I'll do it, my daughter says.

Sangju is usually a man. Don't you have any men around?

I am reminded of my daughter's situation again as my face turns red.

What does it matter if it's a man or a woman? Lane chimes in. There's no law against it.

The employee looks at me. I nod. The thought that my sad, pathetic situation has been exposed once again tears through me. I walk down the hall of small funeral rooms packed in together and go outside. Apart from the two by the entrance, all the rooms are dark and empty. I stand by the window and look out onto the unnecessarily spacious parking lot. Two trucks covered with green tarps, a few scooters, and a few cars is all I see. I have not heard from Tipat. The foreman told me that he had left a few weeks earlier, and Tipat's co-worker told me a boldfaced lie that he didn't know where he'd gone. It's not important whether that's true or not. Still, will Tipat show up, or won't he? I wonder to myself.

After the sun goes down, the professor's wife and the young newcomer arrive.

This isn't much, but I hope it helps.

The newcomer offers me an envelope because we haven't prepared a contribution box. I tell her this: For the deceased without family or property, the government provides a small sum for funeral costs. I am just happy she's come. But it was awful to see Jen's death treated as work, just a part of someone's endless labor. I confess it was unbearable to see it treated thoughtlessly like an errand to be done.

In the meantime, a few of my daughter and Lane's friends come. Thanks to them, something like a bit of warmth blooms and makes the space cozier.

But in the end, I have to face what I've been dreading all along.

By the way, who's that girl?

I'm in the kitchen taking food out of the containers and onto disposable plates when the professor's wife comes over and asks. I turn toward the refrigerator and mumble, I don't know. Some friend of my daughter's.

I hear she's staying with you.

What on earth did she hear from whom and where? Did my daughter or Lane say something to her? I don't say anything in response even though I know that silence just confirms her suspicion that something is amiss. In the end I clam up as if I'm upset, and step outside.

Here you are. Have you eaten?

In the small smoking booth tucked into the corner of the parking lot, Lane comes looking for me. She sits quietly next to me for a moment. A car pulling out of the lot beams its lights across us as it turns around. Our shadows stretch disproportionately long and then disappear.

The staff from the office wanted confirmation about the funerary procession rite, so I came to ask you. Green says we shouldn't do it, but it's pretty customary. I thought it would be good to do it.

And then Lane adds, I'm sorry. I've been calling her by that name for so long, it's hard to correct it.

I don't say anything.

If it's all right with you, I can help out with the cost.

When I don't say anything, she starts to get up and says, I'll tell them we'll decide tomorrow. There are staff around at night anyway.

Thank you for being here, I manage to say.

Lane stops in a half-standing position, not knowing if she should go back inside or sit back down. I motion her to sit down, and talk to her. I tell her that when someone asks me about her, about her and my daughter, I still don't know what to tell them. Actually, that's not true. I know what to tell them, I know now, but I still cannot say it.

I don't know. I don't know if I'll come to understand you. If such a moment will come in my lifetime.

Lane crushes and bursts the cigarette butts strewn on the ground. The tobacco spills out and stains the cement yellow.

Will I miraculously come to understand you kids? Sometimes miracles don't come in pretty forms. If I don't give up, maybe it'll come at some point. It might. But that requires time. I don't know if I have that much time left.

I mutter to myself.

I cannot say that I understand before that miracle happens. That would be a lie. That would be giving up on my daughter. Giving up on her opportunity to live a proud, normal life. I cannot allow that.

A loud beep comes from the street opposite. The sound quickly zips down the road. Lane only listens. Even so, I cannot bring myself to tell her that I'll try. I don't want to give her false hope. I still have inside me the person who doesn't want to understand anything, the one who wants to understand everything, the one who's watching this from a distance, and so many other versions of me locked in an endless, repetitive battle. I don't have the confidence, energy, or courage to explain it all to her.

A memory comes to me. Long ago, a woman sat before me, head bowed and hands politely gathered on her lap, weeping softly.

I'm sorry, she said. I don't understand why my kid keeps getting into trouble and going down the wrong path.

He just doesn't know better, I said. The day will come when he'll understand how his parents feel.

The best words a teacher can offer parents. Maybe I really believed what I said then. Maybe I was that naive and foolish. He will never come to understand you. He will continue to travel down the wrong path and grow apart from you. No matter what his parents want, he will never return to the place where you want him to be. Even so, none of that will change the fact that he is your child and you are his parent. That fact will never change. Should I have told her that instead?

Would you like to go inside and sleep? You look tired. Lane says after a while.

The professor's wife and the newcomer go home before midnight, and so do my daughter's two friends. In the quiet early morning before dawn, Lane, me, and my daughter sit around a small table. We hold the funerary procession rite before dawn, then the cremation, and when the clerk comes from City Hall, we have to take care of paperwork and other administrative things. We may not get to eat all day. The spicy beef soup has gone cold and a white film of fat sits on the surface. I skim off the fat and have a spoonful. It tastes so salty and spicy that it does nothing to revive my appetite. Still, I mix a lump of rice into the soup and eat it one spoonful at a time.

Eat. Eat up.

I push the boiled pork and kimchi across the table to

them. Lane takes a piece of boiled pork. I bring them a cup of warm water. And I eat every last drop in my bowl.

*

After the meal, I go into the small room prepared for the bereaved. I spread out a blanket that comes with the room and lie on top of it. A pungent smell of incense and the musty smell of dust rise from the blanket. *Tick, tick.* The sounds of the second hand grow clear. I fear if I take a deep breath out, my body will melt away. I close my eyes and try to go to sleep. After this nap, when I wake from a deep, deep sleep, I hope all of this turns out to have been a lie. I hope everything is back to the way it was. An uneventful, easy life that doesn't require any effort to be understood and accepted. But maybe what lies ahead is a life of endless fights and tolerance.

Will I be able to take such a life? Will I get through it?

When I ask myself this question, I see the face of an old woman wearing a stubborn, intractable expression and shaking her head. I close my eyes again. In any case, now is the time for sleep. When I wake up, I will have the energy to get through the next bit of life ahead of me. I am not thinking about what's coming far off in the future, but what I face now. I think to myself that I will only think about what needs to be done today and get it done without incident. All I can do is believe that I will make it through the long stretch of tomorrows.

Jamie Chang is a literary translator. She has translated *Kim Jiyoung, Born 1982* by Cho Nam-joo. She lives in Korea with her wife and dog.